BRIGHT NOTES

TWELFTH NIGHT BY WILLIAM SHAKESPEARE

Intelligent Education

Nashville, Tennessee

BRIGHT NOTES: Twelfth Night
www.BrightNotes.com

No part of this publication may be used or reproduced in any manner whatsoever without written permission, except in the case of brief quotations in critical articles and reviews. For permissions, contact Influence Publishers http://www.influencepublishers.com.

ISBN: 978-1-645425-90-8 (Paperback)
ISBN: 978-1-645425-91-5 (eBook)

Published in accordance with the U.S. Copyright Office Orphan Works and Mass Digitization report of the register of copyrights, June 2015.

Originally published by Monarch Press.
Sandra M. Gilbert, 1964
2020 Edition published by Influence Publishers.

Interior design by Lapiz Digital Services. Cover Design by Thinkpen Designs.

Printed in the United States of America.

Library of Congress Cataloging-in-Publication Data forthcoming.
Names: Intelligent Education
Title: BRIGHT NOTES: Twelfth Night
Subject: STU004000 STUDY AIDS / Book Notes

CONTENTS

1) Introduction to William Shakespeare   1

2) Introduction to Twelfth Night   12

3) Textual Analysis
    Act 1   21
    Act 2   47
    Act 3   74
    Act 4   99
    Act 5   112

4) Character Analyses   128

5) Critical Commentary   140

6) Essay Questions and Answers   146

7) Bibliography   153

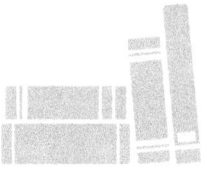

INTRODUCTION TO WILLIAM SHAKESPEARE

FACTS VERSUS SPECULATION

Anyone who wishes to know where documented truth ends and where speculation begins in Shakespearean scholarship and criticism first needs to know the facts of Shakespeare's life. A medley of life records suggest, by their lack of inwardness, how little is known of Shakespeare's ideology, his beliefs and opinions.

William Shakespeare was baptized on April 26, 1564, as "Gulielmus filius Johannes Shakspere"; the evidence is the parish register of Holy Trinity Church, Stratford, England.

HUSBAND AND FATHER

On November 28, 1582, the Bishop of Worcester issued a license to William Shakespeare and "Anne Hathaway of Stratford" to solemnize a marriage upon one asking of the banns providing that there were no legal impediments. Three askings of the banns were (and are) usual in the Church of England.

On May 26, 1583, the records of the parish church in Stratford note the baptism of Susanna, daughter to William Shakespeare.

The inference is clear, then, that Anne Hathaway Shakespeare was with child at the time of her wedding.

On February 2, 1585, the records of the parish church in Stratford note the baptisms of "Hamnet & Judeth, sonne and daughter to William Shakspere."

SHAKESPEARE INSULTED

On September 20, 1592, Robert Greene's A Groats-worth of witte, bought with a million of Repentance was entered in the Stationers' Register. In this work Shakespeare was publicly insulted as "an upstart Crow, beautified with our ["gentlemen" playwrights usually identified as Marlowe, Nashe, and Lodge] feathers, that with Tygers hart wrapt in a Players hyde [a **parody** of a Shakespearean line in II *Henry VI*] supposes he is as well able to bombast out a **blank verse** as the best of you: and being an absolute Iohannes fac totum, is in his own conceit the only Shake-scene in a country." This statement asperses not only Shakespeare's art but intimates his base, i.e., non-gentle, birth. A "John factotum" is a servant or a man of all work.

On April 18, 1593, Shakespeare's long erotic poem "Venus and Adonis" was entered for publication. It was printed under the author's name and was dedicated to the nineteen-year-old Henry Wriothesley, Earl of Southampton.

On May 9, 1594, another long erotic poem, "The Rape of Lucrece", was entered for publication. It also was printed under Shakespeare's name and was dedicated to the Earl of Southampton.

On December 26 and 27, 1594, payment was made to Shakespeare and others for performances at court by the Lord Chamberlain's servants.

For August 11, 1596, the parish register of Holy Trinity Church records the burial of "Hamnet filius William Shakspere."

FROM "VILLEIN" TO "GENTLEMAN"

On October 20, 1596, John Shakespeare, the poet's father, was made a "gentleman" by being granted the privilege of bearing a coat of arms. Thus, William Shakespeare on this day also became a "gentleman." Shakespeare's mother, Mary Arden Shakespeare, was "gentle" by birth. The poet was a product of a cross-class marriage. Both the father and the son were technically "villeins" or "villains" until this day.

On May 24, 1597, William Shakespeare purchased New Place, a large house in the center of Stratford.

CITED AS "BEST"

In 1598 Francis Meres's *Palladis Tamia* listed Shakespeare more frequently than any other English author. Shakespeare was cited as one of eight by whom "the English tongue is mightily enriched, and gorgeouslie invested in rare ornaments and resplendent abiliments"; as one of six who had raised monumentum aere perennius [a monument more lasting than brass]; as one of five who excelled in lyric poetry; as one of thirteen "best for Tragedie," and as one of seventeen who were "best for Comedy."

On September 20, 1598, Shakespeare is said on the authority of Ben Jonson (in his collection of plays, 1616) to have been an actor in Jonson's *Every Man in His Humour*.

On September 8, 1601, the parish register of Holy Trinity in Stratford records the burial of "Mr. Johannes Shakespeare," the poet's father.

BECOMES A "KING'S MAN"

In 1603 Shakespeare was named among others, the Lord Chamberlain's players, as licensed by James I (Queen Elizabeth having died) to become the King's Men.

In 1603 a garbled and pirated *Hamlet* (now known as *Q1*) was printed with Shakespeare's name on the title page.

In March 1604, King James gave Shakespeare, as one of the Grooms of the Chamber (by virtue of being one of the King's Men), four yards of red cloth for a livery, this being in connection with a royal progress through the City of London.

In 1604 (probably) there appeared a second version of *Hamlet* (now known as *Q2*), enlarged and corrected, with Shakespeare's name on the title page.

On June 5, 1607, the parish register at Stratford records the marriage of "M. John Hall gentleman & Susanna Shaxspere," the poet's elder daughter. John Hall was a doctor of medicine.

BECOMES A GRANDFATHER

On February 21, 1608, the parish register at Holy Trinity, Stratford, records the baptism of Elizabeth Hall, Shakespeare's first grandchild.

On September 9, 1608, the parish register at Holy Trinity, Stratford, records the burial of Mary Shakespeare, the poet's mother.

On May 20, 1609, *Shakespeares Sonnets. Never before Imprinted* was entered for publication.

On February 10, 1616, the marriage of Judith, Shakespeare's younger daughter, is recorded in the parish register of Holy Trinity, Stratford.

On March 25, 1616, Shakespeare made his will. It is extant.

On April 23, 1616, Shakespeare died. The monument in the Stratford church is authority for the date.

BURIED IN STRATFORD CHURCH

On April 25, 1616, Shakespeare was buried in Holy Trinity Church, Stratford. Evidence of this date is found in the church register. A stone laid over his grave bears the inscription:

Good Frend for Jesus Sake Forbeare, To Digg The Dust Encloased Heare! Blest Be Ye Man Yt Spares Thes Stones, And Curst Be He Yt Moves My Bones.

DEMAND FOR MORE INFORMATION

These are the life records of Shakespeare. Biographers, intent on book length or even short accounts of the life of the poet, of necessity flesh out these (and other) not very revealing notices from 1564-1616, Shakespeare's life span with ancillary matter such as the status of Elizabethan actors, details of the Elizabethan theaters, and life under Elizabeth I and James I. Information about Shakespeare's artistic life-for example, his alteration of his sources-is much more abundant than truthful insights into his personal life, including his beliefs. There is, of course, great demand for colorful stories about Shakespeare, and there is intense pressure on biographers to depict the poet as a paragon of wisdom.

ANECDOTES-TRUE OR UNTRUE?

Biographers of Shakespeare may include stories about Shakespeare that have been circulating since at least the seventeenth century; no one knows whether or not these stories are true. One declares that Shakespeare was an apprentice to a butcher, that he ran away from his master, and was received by actors in London. Another story holds that Shakespeare was, in his youth, a schoolmaster somewhere in the country. Another story has Shakespeare fleeing from his native town to escape the clutches of Sir Thomas Lucy who had often had him whipped and sometimes imprisoned for poaching deer. Yet another story represents the youthful Shakespeare as holding horses and taking care of them while their owners attended the theater. And there are other stories.

Scholarly and certainly lay expectations oblige Shakespearean biographers often to resort to speculation. This may be very well if biographers use such words as conjecture, presumably, seems, and almost certainly. I quote an example of this kind of hedged thought and language from Hazelton Spencer's *The Art and Life of William Shakespeare* (1940); "Of politics Shakespeare seems to have steered clear ... but at least by implication Shakespeare reportedly endorses the strong-monarchy policy of the Tudors and Stuarts." Or one may say, as I do in my book *Blood Will Tell in Shakespeare's Plays* (1984): "Shakespeare particularly faults his numerous villeins for lacking the classical virtue of courage (they are cowards) and for deficiencies in reasoning ability (they are 'fools'), and in speech (they commit malapropisms), for lack of charity, for ambition, for unsightly faces and poor physiques, for their smell, and for their harboring lice." This remark is not necessarily biographical or reflective of Shakespeare's personal beliefs; it refers to Shakespeare's art in that it makes general assertions about the base - those who lacked coats of arms-as they appear in the poet's thirty-seven plays. The remark's truth or lack of truth may be tested by examination of Shakespeare's writings.

WHO WROTE SHAKESPEARE'S PLAYS?

The less reputable biographers of Shakespeare, including some of weighty names, state assumptions as if they were facts concerning the poet's beliefs. Perhaps the most egregious are those who cannot conceive that the Shakespearean plays were written by a person not a graduate of Oxford or Cambridge and destitute of the insights permitted by foreign travel and by life at court. Those of this persuasion insist that the seventeenth Earl of Oxford, Edward de Vere (whose descendant Charles Vere recently spoke up for the Earl's authorship of the Shakespearean plays), or Sir Francis Bacon, or someone else wrote the Shakespearean plays. It is also argued that the stigma of publication would besmirch the honor of an Elizabethan gentleman who published under his own name (unless he could pretend to correct a pirated printing of his writings).

BEN JONSON KNEW HIM WELL

Suffice it here to say that the thought of anyone writing the plays and giving them to the world in the name of Shakespeare would have astonished Ben Jonson, a friend of the poet, who literally praised Shakespeare to the skies for his comedies and tragedies in the fine poem "To the Memory of My Beloved Master the Author, Mr. William Shakespeare, and What He Hath Left Us" (printed in the *First Folio*, 1623). Much more commonplace and therefore much more obtrusive upon the minds of Shakespeare students are those many scholars who are capable of writing, for example, that Shakespeare put more of himself into Hamlet than any of his other characters or that the poet had no rigid system of religion or morality. Even George Lyman Kittredge, the greatest American Shakespearean, wrote, "*Hamlet*'s advice to the players has always been understood - and rightly - to embody Shakespeare's own views on the art of acting."

In point of fact, we know nothing of Shakespeare's beliefs or opinions except such obvious inferences as that he must have thought New Place, Stratford, worth buying because he bought it. Even Homer, a very self-effacing poet, differs in this matter from Shakespeare. Twice in *the Iliad* he speaks in his own voice (distinguished from the dialogue of his characters) about certain evil deeds of Achilles. Shakespeare left no letters, no diary, and no prefaces (not counting conventionally obsequious dedications); no Elizabethan Boswell tagged Shakespeare around London and the provinces to record his conversation and thus to reveal his mind. In his plays Shakespeare employed no rainsonneur, or authorial mouthpiece, as some other dramatists have done: contrary to many scholarly assertions, it cannot be proved that Prospero, in *The Tempest* in the speech ending "I'll drown my book" (Act V), and Ulysses, in *Troilus and Cressida* in the long speech on "degree" (Act II), speak Shakespeare's own sentiments. All characters in all Shakespearean plays speak for themselves. Whether they speak also for Shakespeare cannot be proved because documents outside the plays cannot be produced.

As for the sonnets, they have long been the happy hunting ground of biographical crackpots who lack outside documents, who do not recognize that Shakespeare may have been using a persona, and who seem not to know that in Shakespeare's time good **sonnets** were supposed to read like confessions.

Some critics even go to the length of professing to hear Shakespeare speaking in the speech of a character and uttering his private beliefs. An example may be found in A. L. Rowse's *What Shakespeare Read and Thought* (1981): "Nor is it so difficult to know what Shakespeare thought or felt. A writer, Logan Pearsall Smith, had the perception to see that a personal tone of voice enters when Shakespeare is telling you what he thinks, sometimes almost a raised voice; it is more obvious again when he urges the same point over and over."

BUT THERE'S NO PROOF!

Rowse, deeply enamoured of his ability to hear Shakespeare's own thoughts in the speeches of characters speaking in character, published a volume entitled *Shakespeare's Self-Portrait, Passages from His Work* (1984). One critic might hear Shakespeare voicing his own thoughts in a speech in Hamlet; another might hear the author in Macbeth. Shakespearean writings can become a vast whispering gallery where Shakespeare himself is heard hic et ubique (here and everywhere), without an atom of documentary proof.

"BETTER SO"

"Closer to truth" is Matthew Arnold's poem on Shakespeare:

Others abide our question. Thou art free. We ask and ask - thou smilest and art still, Out-topping knowledge. For the loftiest hill, Who to the stars uncrowns his majesty, Planting his steadfast footsteps in the sea, Making the heaven of heavens his dwelling Spares but the cloudy border of his base To the foiled searching of mortality; And thou, who didst the stars and sunbeams know, Self-schooled, self-scanned, self-honored, self-secure, Didst tread the earth unguessed at. - Better so. . . .

Here Arnold has Dichtung und Wahrheit - both poetry and truth - with at least two abatements: he exaggerates Shakespeare's wisdom - the poet, after all, is not God; and Arnold fails to acknowledge that Shakespeare's genius was variously recognized in his own time. Jonson, for example, recorded that the "players [actors of the poet's time] have often mentioned it as an honor to Shakespeare, that in his writing (whatsoever he penned) he never blotted a line" (*Timber*), and of course there is praise of Shakespeare, some of it quoted above, in *Meres's Palladis Tamia* (1598).

THE BEST APPROACH

Hippocrates' first apothegm states, "Art is long, but life is short." Even Solomon complained of too many books. One must be, certainly in our time, very selective. Shakespeare's ipsissima verba (his very words) should of course be studied, and some of them memorized. Then, if one has time, the golden insights of criticism from the eighteenth century to the present should be perused. (The problem is to find them all in one book!) And the vast repetitiousness, the jejune stating of the obvious, and the rampant subjectivity of much Shakespearean criticism should be shunned.

Then, if time serves, the primary sources of Shakespeare's era should be studied because the plays were not impervious to colorings imparted by the historical matrix. Finally, if the exigencies of life permit, biographers of Shakespeare who distinguish between fact and guesswork, such as Marchette Chute (*Shakespeare of London*), should be consulted. The happiest situation, pointed to by Jesus in Milton's *Paradise Regained*, is to bring judgment informed by knowledge to whatever one reads.

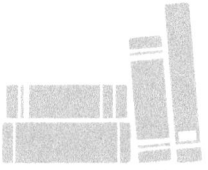

INTRODUCTION TO TWELFTH NIGHT

Twelfth Night, the most carefully plotted and expertly written of Shakespeare's romantic "Golden Comedies" is a miracle of musical form and balance. The festive, gently satirical comic plot centers around a series of practical jokes and mistaken identities, which, in turn, are carried over from the "musical-melancholy" romantic plot. Thus the two plots are inextricably related to each other, while at the same time balancing and counteracting each other in tone and mood. *Twelfth Night*, for which the play was supposedly written (as an entertainment for the Queen's household, according to some recent scholars) was a holiday that came twelve days after Christmas, corresponding to the Feast of the Epiphany. It was a time of rejoicing and holiday high-jinks. Tricks and jokes were the order of the day, and the ordinary rules of life were temporarily suspended. Thus Shakespeare's play deals with human follies-both in thought (vanity, egotism, affectation) and deed (pranks, plots, disguises, mistakes).

SOURCES

Shakespeare's sources for the romantic plot of *Twelfth Night* were one or all of three versions of the same story:

A) an Italian comedy called *G'Ingannati* (The Deceived), first published in 1537 and so popular that by 1585 it had gone through eight Italian editions.

B) a Latin translation of this work (by an English scholar) entitled *Laelia*, which was performed at Queens College, Cambridge in 1950 and 1598.

C) (Most likely) a short tale based on *G'Ingannati* called "The Historie of Appolonius and Silla" and published in 1581 in a collection of such stories, *Farewell to Militarie Profession*, by Barnabe Rich, a popular author of the day.

Most of the distinguishing elements of the romantic plot of *Twelfth Night* - the identical male and female twins, the girl's disguise as a page, her hopeless love for her master, her being forced to "court" her rival, the lady's passion for the girl page, etc. - appear in these earlier versions. The comic plot, however -including the characters of Malvolio, Toby, Andrew, Maria, and Feste, as well as the "gulling" of Malvolio - seems to have been Shakespeare's own addition.

THE TRAGEDIES

Twelfth Night was the last of Shakespeare's "Golden Comedies" and in it his mood was already turning slightly melancholy, as if in preparation for the melancholy atmosphere of Hamlet and the increasing seriousness of his great tragedies. For in the next eight or nine years, from the time when the Lord Chamberlain's men acquired the famous Globe Theatre in 1599 to the time when they moved to Blackfriars in 1608, Shakespeare wrote his greatest masterpieces-*Julius Caesar, Hamlet, Othello, King*

Lear, *Macbeth*, and *Anthony and Cleopatra*, as well as such lesser works as *All's Well That Ends Well*, *Troilus and Cressida*, *Measure for Measure*, *Timon of Athens*, and *Coriolanus*. His vision of the world seems to have darkened in this period, perhaps because of the death of his son (1596), his father (1601), and his mother (1608), and perhaps because of frightening political and social changes which were occurring throughout Europe at this time. His tragedies deal mainly with the flaws of great men who bring destruction on themselves and those around them through their own errors. And in delineating these noble but tragic figures, Shakespeare, like all the world's greatest artists, holds "a mirror up to nature," reflecting in the catastrophic events he depicts, as Francis Fergusson puts it, "the universal meanings he had found in his own and his country's experience."

LAST PLAYS, RETIREMENT AND DEATH

By 1608, when the Lord Chamberlain's Men bought Blackfriars, a new "indoor" theatre, Shakespeare was nearly ready for retirement. His final plays-*Pericles, Cymbeline, The Winter's Tale* and *The Tempest* (especially the latter) - are rich, allegorical works, "Romances" which have little in common with the earlier "Golden Comedies." Serious, sometimes even bitter, they are the mature masterpieces of an artist who has at last come to terms with the mysteries of existence and of his own genius.

After 1610, Shakespeare seems to have spent most of his time in Stratford at New Place. He was undoubtedly a leading citizen of the town, and when he died in 1616 (at the comparatively early age of 52), his will contained a number of substantial bequests. In 1623, the First Folio edition of his complete works was published by a group of his friends as a testimonial to his memory. This was a rare tribute since plays were then considered inferior literature, not really worthy of publication.

A NOTE ON SHAKESPEARE'S THEATRE

The theaters for which Shakespeare wrote-especially the famous Globe Theatre, where the Lord Chamberlain's Men were most permanently based-were very different from our own theaters. Instead of having an indoor "picture-frame" stage, these theaters generally consisted of an unroofed platform (depending on natural daylight for lighting) surrounded on three sides by roofed balconies (where the upper classes could sit and watch) and a lowered floor called "the pit" (where the lower classes, or "groundlings," stood). Because there was no curtain, and no other way to shut off the stage from the audience, there was little or no scenery. For this reason, the playwright had to "set the scene" himself, with his words, and Shakespeare's plays are thus rich in incidental descriptions of the settings where the characters are supposed to be (e.g., "How sweet the moonlight sleeps upon this bank"). In this way Elizabethan audiences were trained to notice all kinds of verbal effects, including, of course, any kind of verbal play, such as puns and slang witticisms. (Much of *Twelfth Night*'s complex verbal wit, and many of the rich poetic effects of its style, then, were indirectly made possible by the nature of Shakespeare's stage.)

BRIEF SUMMARY OF TWELFTH NIGHT

A nobly-born twin sister and brother, Sebastian and Viola, are separated from each other when their ship is wrecked in a storm at sea, and each fears the other has been drowned. Viola, who is rescued by the ship's captain, arrives in the romantic kingdom of Illyria (on the coast of the Adriatic sea) where she decides-for safety's sake-to disguise herself as a boy and seek service with the Duke Orsino, the ruler of the country. This melancholy and rather affected young man has been vainly courting the Countess Olivia, a local lady who has consistently rejected him because of a melodramatic resolve to mourn the recent death of her brother for seven years. Viola, disguised as the boy "Cesario," successfully ingratiates herself with the Duke and is soon sent by him as a messenger-with gift and declarations of love-to his beloved Countess.

In the meantime, we're introduced to several members of Olivia's household, the "low" characters whose antics will advance the comic side of the plot, just as Orsino's, Olivia's and Viola's problems will advance the romantic side. The leader of this group of characters is Sir Toby Belch, Olivia's fat, jolly, hard-drinking cousin, whose love for pranks and merrymaking in general motivates much of the comic action. His companion, Sir Andrew Aguecheek, is a wealthy, skinny, rather feeble-minded knight who has come to Illyria to woo Olivia. Sir Toby encourages his hopeless courtship because he wants Sir Andrew handy for the sake of this money. The three other important comic personages are Maria, Olivia's shrewd servingwoman, who has designs on Sir Toby; Malvolio, her unpleasant, Puritanical steward; and Feste, the household jester, or "Fool."

Viola comes to court Olivia for the Duke, and she does her job with so much grace and wit that the unhappy lady (thinking, of course, that Viola is "Cesario," a handsome young page) falls passionately in love with her. She has her steward Malvolio follow the "boy" with favors and messages. But Viola has herself fallen in love with Orsino, so she's distressed for good reason when she discovers that her rival for his affection, Olivia, harbors a similar passion for her. In the meantime, it turns out that Sebastian, Viola's twin brother, has also been rescued from drowning-by Antonio, a kindly sea-captain, with whom he soon sets out to visit Illyria.

While the romantic triangle of Olivia, Orsino, and Viola is thus stalemated, and before the arrival of Sebastian in town, the comic subplot begins to develop. Sir Toby, Andrew, Feste, and Maria are carousing one night when the priggish Malvolio bursts in to soundly scold them for their merry ways. Determined to revenge themselves and to show up his egotism and pretentiousness, the other comic characters plan to play a practical joke on him by sending him an anonymous love-letter which he'll think is from Olivia herself. They leave the letter in the garden, where Malvolio discovers it when he's strolling already deep in fantasies of being the "Count," Olivia's husband. The unnamed letter-writer (supposedly Olivia) suggests to the egotistical steward that he can become "great" by wooing his lady, the Countess, in yellow-stockings and cross-garters, and by continually smiling at her while at the same time being "surly" with other members of the household. Naturally, the letter fires all his ambitions, and he determines to follow its instructions, instructions which were, however, deliberately designed by Maria to make a fool of him.

Meanwhile, Olivia's own passion for Cesario has become so intense that she openly woos Orsino's "page," much to Viola's discomfort. Indeed, Viola has grown so desperately attached to Orsino that she herself is barely able to keep from confessing her love to him - and when Olivia makes her declaration, she emphatically swears that she can never give her heart to any woman - which is reasonable enough, since she's a woman herself.

At this point, Sebastian and Antonio have arrived in Illyria, and because Antonio once opposed Orsino in a "sea fight," arousing the permanent hostility of the Illyrians, the two decide to separate, Antonio to remain concealed at a nearby inn, and Sebastian to join him there after doing some sightseeing in the town.

By now Malvolio has followed the instructions of the false love-letter, and crazily costumed, he makes a fantastic approach to Olivia, as her wooer. The Countess, supposing him mad-which is just what the plotters intended-gives him into Sir Toby's care to be imprisoned as a lunatic. And with Malvolio "safely" out of the way, she herself once more resumes her own courtship of Viola.

But her favors and attentions to the Duke's "man" have so enraged Sir Toby's friend, the foolish Andrew, that this basically cowardly knight actually challenges "Cesario" to a duel. Though both are anxious to avoid any real fighting (especially, of course, Viola), Sir Toby and Fabian, another of Olivia's servants, egg them on to the point where bloodshed is only avoided by the sudden appearance of Antonio, Sebastian's friend, who, thinking Viola is Sebastian, draws his sword in her defense and ends up battling Sir Toby himself. A group of police officers, however, also appear on the scene and quickly arrest Antonio. The beleaguered captain then asks "Sebastian" (Viola) for a purse he's lent the real Sebastian earlier, and when Viola doesn't know what he's talking about, he accuses her of ingratitude, calling her by her brother's name as the officers lead him away. Viola now realizes that her twin must be alive, and in Illyria, and she goes off in high excitement.

Soon Sebastian himself wanders in and he, in turn, is mistaken for "Cesario" (just as Viola was taken for him) by the clown, Feste, as well as by both Sir Andrew and Sir Toby, who (imagining that he's still as timid as the original "Cesario") attack him once more with their swords. This time, however, they don't find themselves opposed by a young girl with no knowledge of dueling, but by her brother, who spiritedly defends himself and is on the verge of soundly beating them both when Olivia arrives and, like the others, supposing Sebastian to be "Cesario," scolds her cousin for fighting with him and lovingly invites him into her house.

While Sebastian and Olivia are ripening their relationship in one part of the house, Feste, the clown, is persuaded by Maria and Toby to visit the imprisoned Malvolio disguised as "Sir Topas," the priest. After tormenting the unhappy steward for a bit, the jester then returns in his own person - again at the instigation of Toby (who has at last tired of the whole affair) - and provides Malvolio with pencil and paper so he can write to Olivia informing her of his plight.

In the meantime, Olivia persuades Sebastian, who's fallen in love with her quickly enough, to marry her at once. She still thinks, of course, that he's "Cesario," and not trusting his sudden apparent change of heart, wants to make certain of him while she can. Sebastian is aware that there must be some mistake in all this, but he decides that, even if he's mad or dreaming, Olivia is a beautiful hallucination and he, too, will take advantage of the opportunity the moment brings.

At last Orsino, accompanied by Viola and his entire retinue, visits Olivia to renew his suit in person. There he encounters Antonio, who again claims that Viola, as Sebastian, has mistreated him - and when Olivia appears, to the Duke's surprise and anger, she addresses "Cesario" as husband. Viola, of course, denies both Antonio's and Olivia's accusations, but the priest who married Olivia and the other "Cesario" (Sebastian) supports the Countess's claim. Orsino is ready to banish or condemn Viola, when Andrew and Toby also appear with a complaint; they accuse "Cesario" of having beaten them. Viola again denies all knowledge of the affair, but she seems to have become a general object of blame when Sebastian himself at last appears onstage, and all the complications are satisfactorily resolved.

It's clear, of course, that he, and not Viola, is responsible for Andrew's and Toby's injuries. The twins are reunited. Olivia discovers that, after having unluckily fallen in love with the sister, she's luckily married the brother. Antonio learns that Sebastian had kept faith with him after all. And finally Orsino, finding that his devoted "page" is really a woman, decides that he can easily return her devotion and lovingly proposes to the happy girl.

In the midst of all this rejoicing, Olivia remembers Malvolio, and after Feste has given her the steward's letter, outlining his grievances, the miserable man himself is brought in to have the secret of his "madness" - Maria' letter - explained by Fabian. Fabian also reveals that Sir Toby has rewarded the servingwoman for her cleverness by marrying her, and when Malvolio - still as nasty as ever, despite the lesson he's been taught - rushes off in a rage to seek his revenge, the rest of the party is left onstage to plan a celebration of the three marriages which bring *Twelfth Night* to its joyous conclusion.

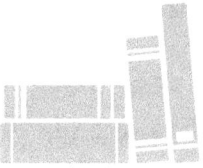

TWELFTH NIGHT

TEXTUAL ANALYSIS

ACT 1

ACT 1: SCENE 1

The play opens in a room in the palace of Orsino, the Duke of Illyria. Orsino is attended by his gentlemen-in-waiting, Curio and other lords.

Comment

Though Illyria was, in fact, a place on the east coast of the Adriatic sea in Europe, Shakespeare was just using the name to give an exotic flavor to what was really an imaginary kingdom. Like most Elizabethan dramatists, Shakespeare was fond of setting his romantic comedies in "faraway places with strange sounding names." He never tried to make these places realistic by introducing "local color, "but just used them to create an air of magic and make-believe. The tradition of setting romantic comedies in such exotic locales persists to this day, as in Shaw's *Arms and the Man* or, more recently, Peter Ustinov's *Romanoff and Juliet.*

Grouped about the stage are musicians, who have been entertaining Orsino and his company with airs played on the lute (a Renaissance stringed instrument, very like a large mandolin), recorder (a primitive flute), and other Elizabethan instruments. Orsino's first speech is one of the most famous in the play. "If music be the food of love, play on," he orders his musicians. "Give me excess of it, that, suffering,/ The appetite may sicken and so die." What he's actually saying in this speech is: "If love is nourished by music, play more than enough music indeed, play too much of it so that my appetite for music (and, perhaps, by extension, for love) will become jaded, and I'll no longer be bothered by the romantic longings that plague me now!"

It seems that Orsino is desperately in love with Olivia, a noble-woman of the country, but has so far been rejected in his suit, mainly because Olivia is determined to mourn the recent death of her only brother for a seven-year period. Orsino, in a vain attempt to forget his frustrated courtship, has been listening to music. Hence his comments on the subject. But he almost immediately tires of the tune the musicians play and remarks on how "quick and fresh" is the spirit of love, always longing for change and distraction, always restless and unsatisfied.

Comment

The structure and language of this first speech are quite complicated, showing, right at the outset, that the Shakespeare of *Twelfth Night* had advanced beyond the straight-forward, though lavishly ornamented, writing of his earliest comedies and history plays, and was moving toward the more difficult style of his middle period, the period of the major tragedies. *Hamlet*, after all, with all its complexity, is believed to have been written shortly after *Twelfth Night* (in 1601 or 1602), and *Twelfth Night* like *Hamlet*, abounds in paradoxes (unusual turns of thought), conceits, puns and other word play. Conceits (extended **metaphors** or comparisons between several different objects or qualities) are especially evident in Orsino's speeches in this scene. Music, love, and food, for example, are compared to each other in the first few lines of the scene.

Curio asks Orsino if he wants to go hunting-perhaps to distract him further from his romantic melancholy, since music no longer entertains him-but Orsino turns aside the question with a pun on "hart" (a stag) and "heart" and with the comparison of his desires to "cruel hounds." A moment later, Valentine, another of Orsino's servingmen, enters with news that Olivia has refused to hear Orsino's latest message of love, on account of her resolve to mourn her brother for seven years. She's even resolved, Valentine reports, not to leave her house during this mourning period!

Orsino, surprisingly, is pleased by this. If Olivia is capable of such devotion to a brother, he reasons, how devoted a wife or mistress will she be when her desires are channeled in more romantic directions. And taking heart from this thought, Orsino closes the scene in a manner typical of Shakespeare's early romantic comedies, with an exuberant **couplet**: "Away before me to sweet beds of flowers! Love - thoughts lie rich when canopied with bowers!"

SUMMARY

1. This short (41 lines) scene introduces one of the major characters of the play, Orsino, Duke of Illyria, and reveals his character, at the outset, as a self-pitying, rather affected lover, who is probably more in love with love than he is with the lady Olivia.

2. The scene also introduces, though not in person, another of the play's major characters-Olivia. Even though we don't actually see Olivia, we learn a lot about her personality from Valentine's report of her decision to mourn her brother for seven years. We learn, for instance, that she's intense in her affections and rather inclined to extravagant, almost melodramatic gestures. In this way, she's much like Orsino - self-absorbed and perhaps a bit affected.

3. Orsino's romantic sadness, which this scene depicts, is part and parcel of his frustrated love for Olivia, but it also strikes, at the very beginning of the first act, what is to be one of the major notes of the play - the note of melancholy. The three major serious characters of the play, Orsino, Olivia, and Viola, (as opposed to the "low" or comic characters, Maria, Sir Toby, Sir Andrew, Malvolio, etc.), are pretty consistently melancholy throughout *Twelfth Night*. (a) Orsino is melancholy because he's so hopelessly in love with love; (b) Olivia is melancholy because, at least at first, she's so much in love with the idea of perpetual grief; and (c) Viola is melancholy, as we shall see, because she's forced to conceal her true nature and her love for Orsino.

4. With its mention of music in the first line, this scene introduces another especially significant element of the play-music. Between references to music and the actual use of music-in important songs, background music, etc. - *Twelfth Night* is one of Shakespeare's most musical works. It's even musical in its structure, with contrasting **themes** and personalities "played" against each other, and in the consistently elegant language of its serious characters.

ACT 1: SCENE 2

We're now at the seashore, where Viola, a nobly-born young girl (who, with Olivia, is one of the play's two heroines) appears with a sea-captain and some sailors. Bewildered, she asks the captain what country they are in, and he tells her that this is Illyria. It turns out that she and her twin brother, Sebastian, had been traveling in this same captain's ship when it was wrecked in a storm off the Illyrian coast. Viola wonders despairingly whether her brother has been drowned, and the captain remarks that since she has been saved by chance (in a lifeboat, with the captain and sailors who accompany her now), her brother may also have been saved by chance. In fact, he reports, as the ship was going down he noticed that her brother, being "most provident in peril," had skillfully bound himself to a floating mast, and in his opinion there's every reason to hope that Sebastian may thus have been saved. Viola promptly rewards him for this piece of encouragement with some gold, and then proceeds to cross-examine him about Illyria-who rules it, whether he's married or single, what sort of lady he's courting, etc.

Comment

Viola's practical energy - the vigorous way in which she sets about figuring out ways to improve her situation - contrasts favorably with Orsino's languid melancholy. Moreover, her sensible reaction to what appears to be the loss of her brother contrasts favorably with Olivia's melodramatic grief. Indeed, the fact that Viola's name is a near perfect anagram (rearrangement of the letters) of Olivia's name, is interesting to consider. It suggests that the two girls, whose lives seem to parallel each other, may represent two different aspects of the female character.

Viola learns from the captain that Orsino, the Duke of Illyria, is hopelessly in love with Olivia, who will not admit his suit because she's in mourning. At first, Viola expresses a desire to serve Olivia. As a well-born young girl, she would obviously be in the safest and most respectable position in the household of a wealthy Illyrian countess. But when the captain tells her that the grieving Olivia will see no one, she swiftly decides that her next best sanctuary, while waiting news of her brother, would be Orsino's own court. Prudently, however, she resolves that the captain should present her to Orsino, not as a helpless and unprotected maiden, but as a "eunuch," a boy-singer, who can entertain him "with many sorts of music."

Comment

Having the heroine disguise herself as a boy was a favorite device in Shakespearean romantic comedy. One reason for its prevalence, of course, was that all the female parts in Elizabethan plays were taken by young boys anyway, since the life of the stage was considered unsuitable for respectable women. But perhaps an even more important reason for the use of this plot-device was the amusing cases of mistaken identity which it made possible. As we shall see, the **denouement** (solution) of *Twelfth Night* depends on just such a case of mistaken identity.

Having already learned of Orsino's fondness for music in scene 1, we can imagine how much of a hit the graceful and talented Viola will be with him, even in the guise of a boy. As the scene closes, she and the captain are setting out, with high hopes, for his court.

SUMMARY

1. From this scene we learn how and why Viola, and later, her brother Sebastian, have come to Illyria.

2. More important, we are introduced here to the charming Viola who, with Olivia and Orsino, is one of the play's three main serious characters. Her good sense, optimism, and energy are shown in striking contrast to the languid affectations of Orsino and Olivia, which we encountered in the last scene.

3. Viola's resolve, at this point, to disguise herself as a boy is to become one of the turning points of the plot later on.

4. The fact that she will also be a musician continues the emphasis on music, which was already introduced as a significant element of the play in the first scene.

ACT 1: SCENE 3

A room in Olivia's house. As the scene opens, Olivia's uncle, Sir Toby Belch, and her serving-maid, Maria (really a kind of lady-in-waiting), enter in the midst of a heated discussion. Sir Toby Belch-as his name suggests, a fat, jovial, middle-aged lover of food, drink, and all the other good things in life-complains about Olivia's excessive grief for her brother. Her insistence on prolonged mourning has cast a pall over the whole household, and Toby is annoyed that anything should interfere with his usual pleasures.

Comment

In Sir Toby Belch, Shakespeare was creating another character like the popular Sir John Falstaff, who was such a hit in *Henry IV*, parts I and II. Like Falstaff, Toby is a plump knight with a great fondness for merrymaking of all kinds. Indeed, although the main comic characters of *Twelfth Night*-Sir Toby, Sir Andrew Aguecheek, Maria, Malvolio and Feste-are supposedly "Illyrians," they are all really, like Falstaff, caricatures of some of the representative personality types of Elizabethan England-e.g. the jolly knight (Sir Toby), the weak-minded coward (Sir Andrew), the clever, flirtatious servant (Maria), etc.

Maria reproves Sir Toby for his wild behavior. Olivia wishes he would come in earlier at night, she tells him, and she herself, Maria, certainly agrees that he should "confine" himself "within the modest limits of order." Moreover, neither she nor her lady, she adds, think very much of his friend, Sir Andrew Aguecheek, a "foolish knight" whom Sir Toby has introduced into the household as a suitor for his niece. "He's drunk nightly, in your company," Maria complains, besides being stupid, quarrelsome, and cowardly, a most unpromising combination!

Sir Toby defends his friend, insisting that he has 3000 ducats a year (a handsome income), plays the viol-da-gamba (ancestor of the modern cello), and speaks three or four languages "word for word without book!" Of course, these last two claims are really outrageous, as Maria knows, and as the audience learns when, a minute later, Sir Andrew himself appears. His behavior during the rest of the scene is so simple-minded that no one could possibly believe in Sir Toby's statements about him.

There is much comical word-play, at this point, between Maria, Sir Toby, and Sir Andrew-although the latter's participation is mainly unconscious. For instance, Sir Toby suggests that he should "accost" Maria, meaning that he should flirt with her, but Sir Andrew misunderstands him and, thinking he's introducing Maria by name, addresses her as "Good Mistress Accost!"

Comment

A good deal of Shakespeare's humor depends on this kind of word-play, which is often hard for a modern audience to follow, since so much of it depends on a knowledge of words whose meaning is now obscure. However, some modern humor which we do appreciate-such as that of the Marx Brothers, for instance-is really identical in origin. Compare this exchange from Duck Soup:

Minister: Your excellency, I propose we take up the tax.

Groucho: Well, I propose we take up the carpet.

Minister: But I insist that first we take up the tax.

Groucho: You know, he's right. You've got to take up the vacs before you can take up the carpet! with the following exchange between Sir Toby and Sir Andrew:

Toby: Accost, Sir Andrew, accost, (meaning "approach her, ingratiate yourself")

Andrew: What's that? (meaning "What's that word mean?")

Toby: (taking "that" to refer to Maria) My niece's chambermaid.

Andrew: Good Mistress Accost, I desire better acquaintance.

Maria: My name is Mary, sir.

Sir Andrew: (continuing the gag) Good Mistress Mary Accost-Such word-play as this will be encountered throughout *Twelfth Night*.

Maria finally gets bored with Sir Andrew's idiocy and flounces out, leaving the two knights alone onstage. Sir Toby accuses Sir Andrew of not being cheerful enough, and Sir Andrew, after some further misunderstanding and silly chatter, confesses that he's about ready to leave for home, since Olivia won't receive him as her suitor. With the Duke himself wooing her, Sir Andrew wonders self-pityingly, what chance can he have? But Sir Toby-who's anxious to have Sir Andrew and his money around a little longer-quickly flatters him into changing his mind.

Comment

With all his stupidity and weakness, Sir Andrew is a colossal egotist, and doesn't find it in the least hard to believe that the beautiful Olivia might prefer a knave like himself to the handsome and highly-placed Orsino.

In any case, Sir Andrew remarks, he loves "masques and revels" and parties of all kinds, and so he'll stay a month longer. At this, Sir Toby asks him jokingly if he likes to dance, and when Sir Andrew replies proudly that he's an expert dancer, Toby sets the foolish knight hopping and skipping around the stage to show off his prowess, meanwhile cracking a series of punning jokes, all of which are lost on the dancing Andrew. As they exit, Sir Toby is crying, "Let me see thee caper: ha! higher: ha, ha! excellent!" and his friend is executing a series of mad leaps and pirouettes.

SUMMARY

1. This scene introduces us into Olivia's household, where we meet three of the most important "low" characters of the play-Sir Toby Belch, Sir Andrew Aguecheek, and Maria-who will be of the greatest importance in forwarding the comic side of the action.

We learn (a) that Olivia disapproves of her uncle Toby's behavior - and this sheds further light on her character, as well as on Toby's; (b) how and why Sir Andrew happens to be on the fringes of Olivia's household; and (c) how both Toby and Maria feel about Sir Andrew. Toby is patronizing- but out to get all he can in the way of money and merry-making from the gullible knight. Maria is contemptuous and disapproving.

2. This is the first strictly comic scene of the play. It's written in prose, unlike scenes 1 and 2, which were entirely in **blank verse** (unrhymed lines of poetry with each having five iambic feet). Prose is one of Shakespeare's principal ways of differentiating comic

characters from serious characters in all he plays, but in addition it serves to effectively change the pace from one scene to the next. Thus, prose scenes like this one between Toby, Maria, and Andrew will provide "comic relief" from the more lyrical speeches of Viola, Orsino, and Olivia throughout *Twelfth Night*.

3. At the end of this scene, the three main elements of the plot have been set in motion: the one stemming from the relationship of Orsino and Olivia; the one resulting from the shipwreck of Viola and Sebastian, and the one relating to Maria, Toby, and the other members of Olivia's household. By the time *Twelfth Night* is over, these three story-lines will have been so skillfully interwoven that they'll seem like one.

ACT 1: SCENE 4

Scene 4 takes place at Orsino's court, where Viola is already well-established in the guise of Cesario, the Duke's favorite pageboy. Wearing man's attire, she enters deep in conversation with Valentine, one of the attendant lords we met in scene 1. If the Duke continues to treat you so well, Valentine tells Viola wonderingly, "you are likely to be much advanced." It appears that Viola-Cesario, in only three days, has made quite a conquest.

But why do you say "if," Viola asks Valentine? Is the Duke "inconstant in his favors?" When Valentine reassures her that he isn't, she thanks him, and they turn to greet Orsino himself, who has just entered with Curio and some of his other servants.

Comment

Orsino's immediate attraction to Viola, even in the role of the boy Cesario, foreshadows his ready acceptance of her as a wife at the end of the play. Indeed, the fact that he first learns to cherish her as a kind of young male protégé helps her - though she doesn't realize it - to win her way slowly into his affections at a time when his fancied love for Olivia would have prevented him in any case from paying much attention to her as a woman.

As if to confirm Valentine's words, Orsino immediately calls for Cesario-Viola, and orders the other servingmen away. Alone with Viola, he reminds her that she now knows everything there is to know about him. To her, in the guise of Cesario, he has "unclasped ... the book even of [his] secret soul." For this reason, she's most suitable, he thinks, to act as an envoy from him to Olivia, bearing his messages of love and courtship. When Viola protests that if Olivia is so "abandoned to her sorrow" (for her brother) as she's said to be, "she never will admit me," Orsino urges her to be "clamorous" and rude, if necessary, rather than return unheard. He's sure, he continues, that if Viola is admitted, his suit will be more acceptable to Olivia if presented by an attractive youth like herself than from an older messenger "of more grave aspect."

Indeed, Orsino tells Viola, unconscious, of course, of the truth of his words, she (Cesario) hardly seems like a man at all. The goddess Diana doesn't have any softer or rosier lips than this "serving boy," he thinks, and even Cesario's voice is like a girl's. But the only lesson he draws from all this is-not that Cesario is a girl (he could hardly believe that) - but that since she (he) seems so feminine, her youth and gentleness are likely to be quite successful with the melancholy Olivia, whose delicate emotional state might be upset by a coarser, more masculine messenger.

Comment

This is an important speech because it shows, like Valentine's speech earlier, that even in the guise of a boy Viola has proven most attractive to Orsino - and not just because of her pleasant personality. Indeed, if we didn't know that Orsino was ostensibly addressing his page, we'd think his words here sounded almost like those of a lover, especially when he compares Viola's lips to the goddess Diana's. It's ironic, from the audience's point of view-as well as Viola's - that the Duke should have sensed so much about this "boy" Cesario, and guessed, in fact, so little.

Orsino finishes his speech to Viola by sending "some four or five" attendants with her - a good company - and commenting self-pityingly that "I myself am best/ When least in company." "I'll do my best/ To woo your lady," Viola promises - and then surprises us by remarking, in an aside to the audience, that here is a "barful strife" (a difficult situation), since, no matter what wooing she does for Orsino, she herself would like to be his wife.

Comment

This is the first intimation we have that in her three days at court, Viola has not only managed to attract the favors of Orsino, but also, most unhappily (from her point of view), to fall in love with him herself. Now she finds herself in a difficult position indeed: on the one hand, as Cesario, the Duke's most trusted servingman, she must be loyal to her master and see to it that his courtship of Olivia prospers; on the other hand, as Viola, an eligible young girl-attractive and of good family-who is herself in love with Orsino, the last thing in the world that she wants is for her beloved to be successful in his wooing of another woman.

SUMMARY

In this short scene we learn:

1. That the Duke finds Cesario-Viola both personally congenial and physically attractive. Though he believes her to be a boy, he has already recognized her femininity - and this prepares the way for him, in act 5, to make her his "mistress and his fancy's Queen."

2. We learn also that Viola, in only three days, has more than reciprocated Orsino's feelings of friendship. Since no misunderstandings or disguises mar her view of him, she's fallen head over heels, in love with him-something he can't do with her until he learns that she's not really a boy!

3. One of the most important elements of the romantic plot - the relationship between Olivia and Viola - is set in motion when Orsino decides to send Cesario as a messenger to his lady.

ACT 1: SCENE 5

Scene 5 returns us to Olivia's house, where we're finally going to meet that much talked-of lady. But before her entrance, Maria, her servingwoman, appears in the act of administering a sound scolding to Feste, the household fool, a character now being introduced for the first time.

Comment

Most upper-class sixteenth-century households contained, of course, a number of servants and retainers of all kinds - scullery maids, servingmen, stewards, ladies-in-waiting, etc. - and among these was almost always included a fool, a witty, clownlike entertainer who, besides providing formal entertainment in the way of songs and performances on the lute or other instruments, could amuse the family with a steady stream of clever repartee. Shakespeare, whose plays are full of the kind of verbal wit that fools specialized in, made extensive use of such clown-figures in many of his most important works. Often, and especially in *King Lear*, the fool's seemingly careless words are shown to embody a higher, paradoxical kind of wisdom - and even in a comedy like *Twelfth Night*, as we shall see in this scene, the fool's humor occasionally has serious overtones.

It seems that Feste, the fool, has been missing from the household more or less "without leave" for some time - and "my lady will hang thee for thy absence," Maria mockingly threatens him. "Let her hang me," replies Feste with good-humored defiance, "he that is well hanged in this world needs to fear no colors." This last sentence embodies a pun on "colors," "collars" and "cholers" - all three of which were pronounced alike in Shakespeare's day, and thus means more or less "Let her do her worst; once she does, I'll have nothing more to fear!"

Comment

Such complex puns are typical of the Shakespearean fool's wit, and they will be encountered throughout *Twelfth Night*. Actually, however, although the fool may produce a greater number of puns of this kind than the other comic characters, his essentially verbal humor is no different from the similarly verbal with which we already noted in the earlier scene (Act 1, scene 3) between Maria, Sir Toby, and Sir Andrew Aguecheek.

Maria continues to scold the fool for his unwarranted absence - and Feste continues to turn away her wrath with light answers. After a few more attempts at seriousness, she can't help falling in with his mood, since she herself is an eminently fun-loving creature - and finally he compliments her by saying that "If Sir Toby would leave drinking" she'd be "as witty a piece of Eve's flesh as any in Illyria" - that is, as clever and high-spirited a mistress as Sir Toby, were he so inclined, could hope to find. But this strikes too close to home, and Maria, embarrassed, hushes Feste with an impatient "Peace, you rogue" - and before he has a chance to tease her any more, Olivia herself approaches, with her steward, Malvolio.

Comment

The fool's teasing words are the first hint we have - and one of the only ones we ever get - that there's "something up" between Maria and Sir Toby. Indeed, although there's always a flirtatious air about Maria - and although Sir Toby often expresses his admiration for her - their eventual marriage is probably the biggest surprise in the play.

As Olivia enters, Feste nervously addresses her - but, deep in her grief, she abstractedly orders her servants to have "the fool" removed. "Do you not hear, fellows? Take away the lady!" Feste remarks - and, before Olivia can repeat her order, he manages to prove that she, and not he, is the fool, with his ready with easily transforming an uncomfortable situation into an apt setting for his light-hearted talents. She's a fool, he points out, in a perfect

parody of learned argument, to mourn for her brother's soul being in heaven -the implication being, of course, that she should rather rejoice at her brother's good fortune in being among the blessed.

Olivia is pleased by his "proof" - and turning to her sour-faced steward, Malvolio, asks what he thinks of the fool. "Doth he not mend?" (that is, mend or heal her sorrow). Malvolio answers with a scornful remark about Feste's abilities, and about fools in general, and there's a rather bitter exchange of words between the two retainers, ending with Malvolio contemptuously calling Feste a "barren" (untalented) "rascal" who could easily be "put down" by "an ordinary fool that has no more brain than a stone."

Comment

This is our introduction to Malvolio, and he displays the essence of his character at once, in his first few speeches in this scene. He's rather Puritanical (though there is some disagreement as to whether or not he actually is a Puritan), an arrogant, humorless, "self-made" man, with ambitions to lift himself above the servant class of which he's still a part. Consequently, as in this scene, he takes every opportunity to heap scorn on the "lighter" people of the household-Feste, Maria, the servant Fabian, and even Sir Toby and Sir Andrew who, though of a better class, seem to more naturally belong with the roistering retainers than with dignified fellow aristocrats like Olivia and Orsino. The idea is certainly inescapable that in Malvolio Shakespeare intended to mercilessly satirize those members of the rising Elizabethan middle class who behaved in such a prim and proper, pleasure-hating way. And Malvolio's characteristically nasty crack about Feste in this scene inspires, as we shall see, the hilarious subplot on the part of Feste and his friends to bring about the arrogant steward's downfall.

Olivia, who, as a born aristocrat, is easier with fools and servants than Malvolio can ever be (since she doesn't have such a need to constantly prove how superior she is to them) responds most perceptively to his attack on Feste. "You are sick of self-love, Malvolio," she remarks-sensing instinctively the monstrously inflated egotism that leads him to behave as he does - and goes on to point out that the "generous, guiltless" and innocent mind isn't so sensitive to imaginary insults, or to the kind of barbed witticisms that a fool like Feste specializes in. People like herself, she implies, who are easy with themselves and with their society, understand that there's never any real harm in such fellows.

Feste, relieved, thanks her for her kindness, and a moment later Maria (who had rushed offstage after her last embarrassing exchange with him) re-enters to announce that a young gentleman (Viola-Cesario) has appeared at the outer gate, demanding to see Olivia. Olivia asks if he comes from Orsino, and Maria replies that she doesn't know, but that "Tis a fair young man, and well attended" - so evidently Viola's good looks make an impression everywhere she goes. When Olivia hears that only her "mad" cousin Toby has remained behind to keep this mysterious messenger out, she dispatches Maria to "fetch him off" - and Malvolio, who, for all his arrogance, can be trusted (she thinks) to handle a delicate matter, is sent to dismiss the young "man."

A moment later, Sir Toby, having been called away from the gate by Maria, enters, belching and half-drunk. Olivia, distressed (though good-humoredly so) gently scolds him, and then engages in a bit of dialogue with Feste about the similarity of a drunken man to "a drowned man, a fool and a madman." Finally, she orders Feste to look after her cousin, and he obediently leads Sir Toby off, commenting humorously that "the fool [himself] shall look to the madman [Toby]."

The moment these two are gone, Malvolio reappears with word that Orsino's young envoy will not allow himself to be dismissed. Curious, Olivia asks, "What kind o' man is he?" and Malvolio replies-with hilariously scornful vagueness - "Why, of mankind." But on being pressed by Olivia, he admits in more specific terms that the Duke's messenger is indeed quite young and very good-looking. Really intrigued by now, Olivia decides to "let him approach," and calls for Maria to come in and give her veil. Thus attired-disguised almost-she prepares to "once more hear Orsino's embassy."

Now Viola enters, in the costume of Cesario of course, and confused by the group of veiled ladies who greet her (Maria and Olivia's other attendants have also veiled themselves) she asks for the lady of the house. Olivia responds-but Viola, still uncertain, asks in the most charming way for further assurance that she's indeed addressing the right person. She's worked hard studying her speech, she tells the ladies frankly, and besides she's very sensitive to "ill usage." When Olivia once again reassures her of her identity, Viola continues her wooing, but with many comically candid asides-such as "I will on with my speech in your praise, and then show you the heart of my message." When both Olivia and Maria grow slightly impatient with the youthful ambassador's long-windedness and urge her to get to the point or "be gone," Viola begs Olivia to dismiss Maria and her other attendants and allow her (Viola-Cesario) to address her (Olivia) in private. Amused - and perhaps more than amused, rather charmed - by this unconventional "fellow," Olivia complies, and the two are left alone onstage.

Now then, Olivia asks, "What is your text?" Viola immediately launches into her prepared speech - "Most sweet lady" - but is interrupted by Olivia. After a moment of witty banter between the two, Viola, overcome by curiosity about Olivia (who is, after all, though she doesn't realize it, her rival for Orsino's love) asks to be allowed to see her face, which has remained veiled throughout the interview. Obligingly (still intrigued by the young messenger), Olivia removes the veil and asks if Viola-Cesario doesn't think her face is "well done." "Excellently done," replies Viola dryly, "If God did all" - that is, if it's natural and not a product of artificial making-up, etc.

Comment

This rather cynical humorous remark, as well as her other witty lines scattered throughout this scene, reminds us that Viola - though primarily a serious "romantic" heroine - is more nearly comic than any of the other serious characters in the play. Not only is she naturally high-spirited and of a witty, good-humored turn of mind, but also, as we shall see later, her male disguise leads her into farcical imbroglios (involvements) such as her tangle with Sir Andrew Aguecheek, which aren't possible for Olivia and Orsino, the more dignified hero and heroine.

When Olivia assures Viola that her beauty is indeed natural, Viola-perhaps a little bit envious, and more than a little depressed at having to contend with such a rival when the man she loves isn't even aware of her existence as a woman yet-waxes rhapsodic about Olivia's looks. Olivia, she says, is "too proud" but "if you were the Devil, you are fair" - and she goes on to press Orsino's suit, remarking that she can well imagine why her lord and master is in love with such an incomparable beauty.

Olivia, who, by now, is much less interested in the master than in the "man," replies coldly that Orsino knows her mind very well. Though she's aware of all his virtues and advantages, she cannot love him, and "he might have took his answer long ago." But Viola responds that she still understands how her master feels-since if she were in his position she wouldn't take no for an answer either. What would you do? Olivia asks - and she replies, in a famous speech, that she would make herself "a willow cabin" at Olivia's gate (that is, camp at Olivia's door), and call upon her soul within the house (swear solemn oaths of fidelity); write songs of love, and sing them even in the dead of night; shout Olivia's name to the hills, until all the air re-echoed it, etc.

Comment

This wonderfully lyric speech reinforces our idea of Viola as a serious "romantic" character - so that we've seen both sides of her personality within the space of this short interview with Olivia. Certainly we can understand why Olivia should feel so attracted to so magically attractive and persuasively fluent a young "man" - and certainly we may suspect that much of the passion with which Viola's language is infused is more a result of her own lonely passion for Orsino than of any deeply felt loyalty to him as Olivia's suitor.

When Viola has finished speaking, Olivia comments meaningfully that "you might do much" - and then, unable to repress her interest in this mysteriously attractive messenger, asks her briefly about her family background (a sure sign that she's regarding the young envoy as "himself" a potential suitor). Viola replies that her background is even better than her present position as a servant implies (which indeed it is), but that at least she's "a gentleman." Relieved, Olivia dismisses her-remarking that she might as well tell Orsino that there's no hope for his suit-but quickly adding, rather slyly, that of course Cesario (the messenger) might return to tell her how Orsino takes her reply. She then adds insult to injury by offering Viola a purse full of gold, which Viola scornfully rejects, promptly departing with an angry "Farewell, fair cruelty."

Olivia is left alone onstage to meditate aloud, in a short soliloquy, on "this youth's [Cesario's] perfections." With some trepidation, but a basic fatalistic acceptance, she realizes she's fallen in love with the Duke's messenger - and swiftly deciding to take some action, she calls in the trusted Malvolio, and orders him to follow Viola-Cesario with a ring which, she says, "he" left behind as a token from the Duke (though of course Viola did no such thing) and to tell "him" that if "he'll" return the next day, she'll explain in greater detail why she won't accept it. The whole move is plainly a ruse to get Cesario to come again - and it's just as plainly intended as a flirtatious overture from her to "him," since "he" knows as well as she does that "he" left no ring. When Malvolio is gone, Olivia, alone again onstage, closes the scene by commenting that though she fears she's acting hastily, what is destined to be, must be.

SUMMARY

This long scene accomplishes a number of things in the general context of the play.

1. It introduces Feste, the fool, and gives us some idea of his personality.

(a) He's quick-witted (especially in his dialogue with Olivia), sly (as witness his banter with Maria), merry, and fast to take offense (as we see in his angry exchange with Malvolio).

(b) Not only does his verbal wit provide comic relief throughout the play, but he's a moving spirit in the wickedly funny plot against Malvolio, which the "lighter" people are soon to concoct.

2. Malvolio is also introduced in this scene.

   (a) Through his dialogue with Olivia and the fool, and his behavior with Viola-Cesario, we learn that he's an arrogant, humorless person-a caricature of all that was repulsive to aristocrat and workingman alike in the middle class Puritan - and as such a caricature the character of Malvolio still has validity today.

   (b) His nasty comments to Feste provoke the fool to the point where he's ready to go to almost any lengths to get his revenge-as he does in the next act.

3. We finally meet Olivia in this scene - and we discover that she's just as beautiful, aristocratic and extravagant a personality as she's been said to be. Her beauty is self-evident; her aristocratic spirit is especially manifest in her speech to Malvolio about the fool; her extravagance and impulsiveness are shown by the swiftness with which she falls in love with Viola-Cesario.

4. Viola and Olivia meet for the first time in this scene, making it a central scene in the development of the major romantic plot of *Twelfth Night*, since the relationship-as well as the contrasting personalities-of these two young women is of pivotal importance to the play.

   (a) Knowing the truth about her sex, Viola coolly admires-but is also frankly envious of-Olivia's beauty, especially since she knows herself to be a potential romantic rival of the Illyrian noblewoman's for Orsino's affections.

   (b) Olivia, on the other hand, believing Viola to be Cesario, falls in love almost "at first sight" with her - mostly because of her charm and youthful good looks - thus complicating the plot and preparing the way for its **denouement** (solution) in which she'll marry Sebastian, Viola's twin-brother, who shares the family magnetism.

5. Finally, we learn a little more about Viola in this scene - and with such a delightful heroine, every little bit is interesting.

   (a) We learn, for instance, that she's possessed of a ready, dry wit, as she shows in her quick and capable banter with the proud flirtatious Olivia.

   (b) We learn, too, that she's capable of really lyrical passionate utterances, even on another's behalf - as in her speech to Olivia about what she'd do in Orsino's place - though, of course, much of the intensity of her words may come from her own deep feelings for the Duke.

(c) We also learn that though Viola does her best to loyally carry out her errand for Orsino, her love for him interferes to a certain extent, making her uncontrollably curious about - and ultimately rather envious of - her rival's beauty. Perhaps Olivia mistakes this interest on her part for romantic interest (when it is really female curiosity) and thus is encouraged to fall in love with her!

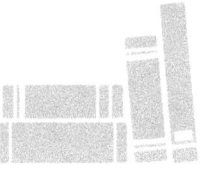

TWELFTH NIGHT

TEXTUAL ANALYSIS

ACT 2

ACT 2: SCENE 1

We find ourselves once more at the Illyrian coast, where a sea captain by the name of Antonio enters in conversation with a very familiar-looking young man-familiar because he's none other than Sebastian, the twin brother after whom Viola has patterned her dress, walk and manner, and about whose fate she's still so painfully uncertain. Antonio begs the young man to stay with him longer (Sebastian has evidently found shelter with this kindly captain after being shipwrecked) and then asks where he plans to go, and whether he (Antonio) may not accompany him. Sebastian replies gloomily that the "stars shine darkly over me" and that he thinks Antonio would therefore be better off without him. As for his destination-he plans merely to wander or, as he puts it, "My determinate voyage is mere extravagancy."

Comment

Sebastian differs slightly from his forthright and down-to-earth sister in that his language tends to be a bit pretentious, and he has a touch more melodrama in his nature-traits perhaps more usually encountered in a young man in his early twenties than in a girl of the same age. (Shakespeare was simply being "true-to-life" in showing the female of the species as a little more mature and practical than her male counterpart). Still, Sebastian-as we can see from the affectionate loyalty he has so quickly inspired in Antonio-shares a good deal of Viola's charm and attractiveness.

Sebastian goes on to reveal his name and noble parentage to Antonio, and to relate how he thinks his twin sister was drowned "some hours" before he himself was rescued (by this same Antonio) from a similar fate. His sister, he continued, was not only beautiful but also intelligent and good, and though she is (he believes) drowned already "with salt water," he is continually drowning her remembrance still more with his salty tears. Antonio is appropriately sympathetic and offers again to accompany the young man, this time as his servant, but Sebastian adamantly refuses, explaining that he is still too grief-stricken and too near tears to be in company. Finally, remarking briefly that he's "bound to the Count Orsino's court," he takes a fond farewell of Antonio and exits.

Antonio, left alone onstage, speculates aloud that he has many enemies in Orsino's court-as we shall see in the next act-or he would certainly follow Sebastian there at once. But he quickly changes his mind, commenting that this young man is so dear to him "that danger shall seem sport" and he will brave whatever obstacles he may encounter in order to accompany his friend to Illyria (even without that friend's knowledge or permission).

SUMMARY

In this brief scene the plot definitely "thickens."

1. We learn for the first time that Sebastian, Viola's twin brother, is still alive.

2. We learn, too, that Sebastian thinks Viola is dead-just as Viola herself thinks Sebastian may be dead - and the fact that both are alive, each supposing the other drowned, will contribute considerably to the plot. Certainly Sebastian's being mistaken by Olivia for Cesario is central to the **denouement** of the story; and Viola's being mistaken by Antonio for Sebastian is also important to the plot, though less crucially than in the case of Sebastian and Olivia.

3. Of course, we also meet Sebastian for the first time and see what kind of person he is.

    (a) He's as attractive and charming as Viola herself might report him to be, as magnetic a personality, in fact, as his twin sister. We can easily see this from the rapidity with which he's won the love and loyalty of Antonio, a kind though (as we are to discover later) warlike and impetuous man.

    (b) Sebastian himself is also tremendously loyal to, and fond of his sister, as we can see from his grief-stricken report of her "death."

4. We also meet Antonio for the first time in this scene, and though he's not going to be of major significance in the play, he is of some importance, especially

the fact that he's impulsively followed his young friend into such hostile territory. This impulsive action of his-plus his quickly conceived affection for Sebastian-illustrates very well the kind but impetuous nature mentioned above. In act 5, Orsino is to accuse Antonio of being a pirate - an allegation which, if true, would accord well enough with the sea captain's hot-headed behavior.

ACT 2: SCENE 2

As this scene opens, Malvolio appears in an Illyrian street near Olivia's house, in hot pursuit of Viola who, as Cesario, has just taken her leave of Olivia in act 1, scene 5. Malvolio is bent, as a matter of fact, on carrying out the errand which Olivia assigned to him at the end of that scene. He comes quickly up behind Viola and asks her if she isn't the same messenger who was just now with the Countess Olivia. When she replies that she is, he contemptuously delivers the ring, which Olivia had told him to give Cesario, scornfully remarking that "you might have saved me my pains, to have taken it away yourself," a nasty comment which the love-struck Olivia hardly instructed him to make. He then adds, as Olivia had told him to, that Cesario should assure Orsino that there's no hope for his suit, but that the messenger might return to report "his" lord's reaction. When Viola replies in confusion that she never gave Olivia any ring, Malvolio angrily responds that of course she "peevishly" threw it to her - and then he himself peevishly tosses the disputed token at Viola's feet, remarking that if it's "worth stooping for, there it lies" - and before the bewildered girl can answer him, he makes his usual "grand" exit.

Comment

Malvolio's behavior in this brief encounter with Viola is as emphatically arrogant as ever. Even in carrying out a minor errand for his mistress, this egotistical steward must show his scorn for all the rest of humanity - all, that is, except those, like Olivia, who are higher placed than he is, and in a position to help him advance himself up the social scale. By now, though we've had little enough to do with him, we, the audience, have come to dislike Malvolio just as heartily as most of the other members of Olivia's household do.

Viola, left alone onstage, exclaims wonderingly that "I left no ring with her. What means this lady?" and then, as the light slowly dawns on her, and she realizes Olivia's romantic intentions, she is by turns amazed, amused, and upset. Obviously, she realizes- despite her own, perfectly cool intentions-her good looks have charmed Olivia, and she recalls that the countess' behavior during their recent interview was indeed rather strange and distracted. Furthermore, since Orsino himself never sent the lady any ring, it's clear, finally, to Viola that the ring is meant as a love gift to her in her guise of Cesario. But what a situation to be in! "Poor lady, she were better love a dream," she muses about Olivia's predicament. As for her own, she comments that she can see that disguise itself is "a wickedness," since it can lead to such ruinous deceptions. But further, she recognizes from this incident that woman's frailty is most of all to blame for problems like this-since the fair sex is so readily susceptible to the first charming countenance that comes along.

Confused, and more than a little upset by the emotional tensions of this increasingly complicated situation, Viola wonders how it will all work out. With Orsino in love with Olivia,

Olivia in love with Cesario, and Viola herself in love with Orsino, things seem to be in a hopeless tangle. Besides, insofar as she is a "man," Viola has to remain loyal to her "master's love" for Olivia - and inasmuch as she's actually a woman, Olivia's love for her must be doomed to disappointment. Finally, the practical Viola simply shrugs and throwing up her hands in mock despair exclaims "O Time, thou must untangle this, not I! It is too hard a knot for me to untie!" Thus rounding out the scene in typical Shakespearean manner with a neat **couplet**, she skips offstage.

SUMMARY

1. Though this scene doesn't introduce any new developments in the plot, it does provide a short (42 lines) pause in which the audience - and Viola - can stop and catch up with the complex interweavings of the action, which until now has been proceeding at a pretty breathless pace.

2. It gives us another look at Malvolio, who is behaving as arrogantly and unpleasantly as ever, even in the course of carrying out a short and simple errand for his mistress. The dislike for him which began to grow in us on his first appearance in act 1, scene 5, is thus reinforced by his rude and contemptuous behavior to the unoffending Viola.

3. We see Viola's gradual comprehension of and reaction to Olivia's mistaken passion for her. Though sympathetic toward the unhappy countess, she remains absorbed in her own love for Orsino, and regards the new development merely as another complication in the tangled situation resulting from her male disguise.

ACT 2: SCENE 3

This scene returns us again to Olivia's house, this time late at night-well after midnight, in fact. Enter Sir Toby and Sir Andrew, both thoroughly inebriated. Jovially, though a bit sleepily and dizzily too, the two knights stagger about the stage, drunkenly discussing the question of whether being up thus-after midnight-is really being up late or being up early (since it's technically already morning). Just as Toby is loudly calling for Maria to bring him some more wine, the fool Feste enters-quite sober compared to the other two, but as witty and high-spirited as ever. He greets the two gaily, and Sir Toby proposes that the three of them sing a "catch" (a kind of round). But before Feste can reply, Sir Andrew, in a wandering, befuddled way (when drunk he's even more foolish and incoherent than when he is sober) begins to elaborately compliment the clown on his recent good "fooling." Amused, Feste thanks him-in typical Shakespearean fool's doubletalk. Sir Andrew, still more pleased and vague, calls for a song, and Sir Toby seconds his motion, offering Feste sixpence to perform, which Sir Andrew promptly doubles with a "testril" (sixpence) of his own.

Comment

It was part of the fool's job to be available a good part of the day or night to entertain various members of the household with his witty remarks or, as now, to divert them with his songs. Of course, he expected to be paid for his efforts - the money which the two knights offer is simply routine - but in *Twelfth Night*, too, he's fond enough of Sir Toby, and amused enough by Sir Andrew, to be a natural companion in their nightly revels anyway.

Having agreed to perform for them, Feste asks Sir Toby and Andrew whether they'd prefer a love song or a song of "good life" (that is, a drinking song). Both drinkers hasten to assure him, quite drunkenly, that there's nothing they'd rather hear than a love song. ("I care not for good life," remarks the carousing Andrew foolishly). The clown rewards their enthusiasm with a melodious rendition of the popular Elizabethan song "O mistress mine, where are you roaming?"

Comment

Shakespeare's songs are among the loveliest Elizabethan lyrics, and the songs sung by Feste and Viola in *Twelfth Night* include some of Shakespeare's best. Often the **theme** of the songs is that love is sweet and life is short, so that lovers ought to, as it were, make hay while the sun shines. Sometimes the mood is sadder, conveying primarily the poignancy and uncertainty of life. Occasionally, the two ideas are combined: life is sad, but love improves it. Certainly all these **themes** are appropriate to a romantic comedy like *Twelfth Night* which emphasizes love and melancholy as much as wit and high spirits. And, of course, this use of music to reinforce the basic emotional tone of the play, is one of the main reasons that *Twelfth Night* is Shakespeare's most musical work. Another reason is that it probably has a higher proportion of songs than any other Shakespeare play, almost every act containing one or more tunes sung by Feste or, in certain productions, Viola, with other characters frequently chiming in too.

When Feste has finished singing, Toby and Andrew join once more to drunkenly compliment him on his sweet voice - and then, a moment later, Toby returns to his original idea that the three revelers should "rouse the night owl in a catch." After some discussion, they decide on a catch known as "Hold thy peace, thou knave," though Feste slyly points out to Andrew that he'll have to call him "knave" (fool) in the course of it. Andrew-who is indeed a knave, or fool-smugly consents, since, as he says, it won't be the first time he's been called a knave. With this, the three set to with a will, singing the noisy and spirited round "Thou knave" at the top of their lungs.

Comment

Andrew's silliness, muddle-headedness, and general foolishness in this scene is eminently in keeping with the behavior he displayed earlier, in Act 1, Scene 3. Though Toby is drunk also, he's much less stupid and vague in his behavior throughout than the consistently "knavish" Andrew.

But after just a few renditions of their song, they're angrily interrupted by Maria, who appears in a doorway, arms akimbo, to scold them in outraged tones for their "caterwauling" which, she threatens, is likely to enrage Olivia to the point where she bids her steward, Malvolio, to "turn" all three culprits "out of doors." Unruffled, the offending threesome begin to chaff and "fool" with Maria herself-Sir Toby especially in a rather flirtatious way. But in another moment, just as Maria had predicted, Malvolio himself arrives, wearing his nightshirt and carrying a candle, in a righteous rage at being wakened in the middle of the night.

Comment

The fact that Malvolio is decked out for bed and was presumably sound asleep at this hour while these other members of Olivia's household are still fully dressed and carousing, emphasizes once more the difference between their attitude toward life and his. Toby, Andrew, Feste, and even Maria are a typically fun-loving group of comic characters, determined to "live it up" and "get the most out of life" whenever possible. Malvolio, on the other hand, is a typical member of the Puritanical new middle class, the kind of man who devoutly believes in such bourgeois saws as "early to bed, early to rise, makes a man healthy, wealthy and wise" and "the early bird gets the worm." Whatever our own personal philosophy may be, it's plain enough from this and other scenes that, in the context of the play, Shakespeare expects his audience to automatically sympathize with the revelers and be repelled by Malvolio's moralistic stuffiness.

Indignantly, Malvolio demands to know what these noisy servants and hangers-on think they're doing here "at this time of night." "Are you mad?" or what? "Do ye make an alehouse of my lady's house?" he asks, in tones of the deepest outrage. "Is there no respect of place, persons, nor time in you?"

His prissily pompous manner naturally infuriates Toby-himself quite drunk and utterly reckless of consequences-who tells him rudely to be hanged, and that as for time, they kept time in their songs. This reply, in turn, enrages Malvolio even more, and he assures Toby that Olivia herself had told him to inform Toby that, unless he could behave himself, she'd "be very willing to bid him farewell" - a threat with some force in it, since Maria had suggested the same thing in her speech earlier.

Comment

Though we're repeatedly told, by both Maria and Malvolio, that Olivia is displeased with her cousin's wild and rowdy behavior in her house, especially since she herself is trying to observe a period of quiet mourning for her brother, it's hard to believe that these threats to turn Toby out are intended as seriously by her as Maria may fear they are, and as Malvolio would like them to be. Certainly her own behavior toward Toby is gentle and good-humored enough. And though we do hear her reprove him for his drunkenness, we never actually hear her scold or threaten him as harshly as Maria and Malvolio say she wants to.

Toby's only response to Malvolio's angry warning is to burst still more rudely and clamorously into song. "Farewell, dear heart, since I must needs be gone," he bellows drunkenly, making fun of Malvolio's dire threats, and though Maria tries to restrain him, the clown joins in and together he two dance and sing around Malvolio in a hilariously insulting duet. Finally, Toby stops singing long enough to ask Malvolio the famous question "Dost thou think because thou art virtuous, there shall be no more cades and ale?"

Comment

These are perhaps the most famous words in the play, and rightly so, since they embody one of the work's central themes. On the comic level, after all, the tension between the Puritanical Malvolio and the roistering Toby is, as we've seen, the play's chief dramatic conflict. Malvolio, the arrogant, rising, moralistic, self-made man threatens Toby - and by implication his whole class, the class of jolly, fat, idle, drunken aristocrats, and its attendant class of idle, drunken, merrymaking servants - with displacement, with "turning out of doors." Not only is he more virtuous than they are, he is also, and most importantly, more efficient. The almost machine-like economy and efficiency even of his speech is to be noted in such pompous but briskly contemptuous utterances as "ye squeak out your cozier's catches without any mitigation or remorse of voice..." Though pretentious, such a style is also condensed and workmanlike, with no room for the kind of time-wasting slang, puns, wit or lyricism in which Shakespeare's more favored characters indulge. Thus Toby's words to Malvolio - "Dost think because thou art virtuous, there shall be no more cakes and ale?" - summarize a whole response, an indignant "Just because you think a lot of your morality, just because you think you're the coming thing, you'd better not expect that the likes of us, with our merrymaking and our love for good food and drink, are going to disappear. We're here to stay too, you know!" - a statement which is, after all, something of an eternal truth, since no matter how hard the virtuous reformers work they can never wholly abolish the pleasure-loving instinct in those of their fellows who are freer and easier with themselves and with life.

Feste - who's only been waiting for a chance to express his pent-up resentment to Malvolio ever since the latter insulted him in front of Olivia in act 1, scene 5 - chimes in too. "Yes, by Saint Anne, and ginger shall be hot i' the mouth too," he shouts, meaning that all the spicy luxuries of life are as eternal as merrymaking itself is. Malvolio - furious and frustrated - turns to Maria, as the only one with whom he has any chance of communicating in this company. Angrily threatening to get her in trouble with her mistress and to report the disorderly conduct of the whole group to Olivia as soon as possible, he stomps off.

Maria-from whom he'd evidently expected a little more respect than the others-rudely shouts after him "Go shake your ears," and when Toby exclaims that maybe he ought to challenge Malvolio to a duel (and then disappoint him by not showing up for it) she unfolds another, cleverer scheme for revenge. If only Toby will be patient for tonight, she says conciliatingly, she'll take care of Malvolio herself as soon as possible. Right now, her mistress is "much out of quiet" - rather upset - because of her recent interview with Orsino's messenger.

Comment

Here's further evidence - if we needed it - that Olivia has indeed fallen passionately in love with Viola - Cesario, since even the light-hearted Maria, always a shrewd observer, has noticed some change, some disturbance, in her usual behavior.

Excitedly, Toby begs to know Maria's opinion of Malvolio, delighted to have found so sly and quickwitted an ally. Well, he's something of a Puritan, Maria begins, rather understating the case. "Oh, if I thought that," exclaims Andrew feebly, "I'd beat him like a dog!" But not only is he Puritanical, Maria continues, he's also affected, ambitious, hypocritical, cold-hearted, and incredibly egotistical. Her revenge, in fact, is to be based especially on this last trait - his egotism - and a devilishly clever scheme it is, too, as Maria outlines it. What she plans to do is to leave an anonymous love letter in a place where Malvolio can easily chance on it, and in which he'll find what seem to be himself described with passion and accuracy. Furthermore, since her handwriting, she explains, is very similar to her mistress', she'll write the letter in such a way that the egotistical steward will believe it to be addressed by Olivia to him. The complications that should ensue from this mistake on his part will, she guarantees, provide "sport royal" for all concerned. Toby and Andrew are delighted, and with a hasty promise to plant them and the fool in a spot where they can observe Malvolio's hilarious "construction" of her letter, Maria rushes off to bed, to "dream on the event."

Left alone onstage, Toby and Andrew remark on Maria's wit and faithfulness to Toby's cause. "She's a beagle, true bred, and one that adores me," comments Toby, not very flatteringly.

> Comment

Evidently, then, Toby himself is as aware as Feste is of Maria's flirtatious inclinations in his direction. This line helps prepare us a little more for the eventual, otherwise rather unheralded romance between the two.

Toby seizes this moment of quiet and relative peace to suggest that Andrew must send for more money. When the foolish knight again expresses doubts that Olivia will have him, Toby reassures him and repeats his demand for money.

> Comment

Charming and jolly as Toby can be, we see in his relationship with Andrew that he definitely has an unscrupulous side to his nature. Perhaps many of Malvolio's objections to him are well-founded—but they're so ill-put that, except in this case of his rather cold-blooded exploitation of a weak-minded friend, we find them hard to credit.

At last the two go off sleepily to drink some more since, as Toby puts it, "tis too late to go to bed now."

SUMMARY

> This rather long and hilarious scene is central to the development of the comic side of the plot, though it

contributes nothing to the serious side (except time in which events can "ripen").

1. It shows us Andrew, Toby and Feste carousing together, as we've heretofore been told they do. They're quite as noisy and objectionable to "decent citizens" like Malvolio as we've been told, too, although they're shown in terms of the play to be basically a rather innocent company of merrymakers.

    (a) Andrew is reintroduced in this scene, and we see he's as foolish and feeble an individual as ever. We also see once more the shameless and rather unscrupulous way in which Toby exploits his interest in Olivia for the sake of his money.

    (b) Feste appears and sings a sweet love song, rather out of keeping with the drunken hilarity of the rest of the scene, but quite in the mood of the rest of the play.

    (c) Toby, of course, is central to the scene - the moving spirit behind all the drunken revels. Falstaffian and hugely frolicsome as ever, it's he who joins with Feste in baiting the Puritanical Malvolio.

2. Maria appears at first as a kind of moderator between the carousing group of hangers-on and the more respectable elements of the household, like Olivia and, especially, Malvolio. She warns Toby that he must stop offending Olivia, and that he and Andrew and Feste must behave themselves more properly. But when Malvolio intervenes, she sides with Toby, showing the side her heart really rests with.

3. Malvolio himself behaves as arrogantly, prudishly and egotistically as ever. He appears only for a few minutes-to soundly scold the others for their behavior-but in those few minutes he manages to be so offensive that:

Maria and the others concoct the plot against Malvolio which is to be the central comic action of the play. Maria, especially, shows her wit and her loyalty to Toby in this scene, since she's the one who's mainly responsible for the devilishly clever scheme to leave a love letter where Malvolio can find it and make him think it was addressed by his mistress Olivia to himself. Only an egotist could make such a mistake, so that ultimately Malvolio himself is responsible for the foolish behavior which this "love letter" is to inspire in him in the next act. It's interesting to note that in this respect there's a parallel between Andrew and Malvolio, neither of whom could possibly ever have a chance with Olivia, but both of whom are driven by colossal egotism to imagine that they do.

4. Though this scene contributes nothing to the serious plot of *Twelfth Night*, it does provide further relief from the romantic developments which have been occurring at such a headlong pace, and it does allow a necessary passage of time in which the various love-relationships (Orsino-Olivia, Olivia-Cesario, Viola-Orsino, etc.) can "ripen."

ACT 2: SCENE 4

We find ourselves again at the palace of Orsino, a place we haven't visited now for quite some time. Melancholy as ever, the lovestruck Duke enters, attended by Viola-Cesario, Curio, and others. As usual, he calls for music, explaining that a certain "old and antique song" he heard last night had "relieved" his "passion much." Songs of the present, he continues, are too brisk and giddy. Curio tells him that Feste, who'd sung the song, is not there right now, and a messenger is dispatched to look for him while Orsino's corps of musicians plays the tune alone.

Comment

Feste, though technically a member of Olivia's household, acts also as a kind of roving entertainer, wandering from one noble house or palace to another, singing his songs and telling his jokes wherever they're called for and wherever he's paid enough for the trouble of traveling to be worth his while.

While they wait for Curio to fetch Feste, Orsino calls Viola-Cesario over to him, remarking, ironically enough, that if she should ever fall in love, he hopes she'll remember his example—for all lovers are just like him, tiring easily and easily bored with everything except the subject of love and the beloved.

Comment

Orsino's remarks to Viola are, from the audience's point of view, ironic, because we know, as he does not, that of the two of them Viola is probably the more deeply and sincerely in love.

The Duke goes on to ask Viola how she likes the melody the musicians are playing, and when she replies gravely that it seems to somehow embody the very spirit of love, he's impressed with the genuineness of her tone, and inquires whether she's ever been in love herself, since she seems to know something about it. Viola replies guardedly that she has. With what kind of woman? Orsino asks. A woman rather like himself, Viola answers, with his coloring and about his age. Distressed (since he himself is a good deal older than Viola), Orsino exclaims that in an ideal relationship, the man should definitely be older than the woman, not vice versa.

Comment

Since Orsino doesn't know that it's really himself Viola is speaking of, and not some mysterious woman, he is upset to think that a young boy like "Cesario" should be in love with an "older woman." If he knew the truth, he'd understand that Viola's thoroughly feminine feeling for himself, an older man, fits all his own requirements for an ideal lovematch.

At any rate, ignorant as he is of the truth of Viola's situation, Orsino goes on to explain that the man should be older than the woman because men are naturally less constant than women, and a man is more likely to grow tired of his wife if she is older than he is. Furthermore, he points out, a woman's beauty, as well as her chastity - the two main traits which make her attractive to a man - is a transient and fleeting thing, like a rose "whose fair flower/ Being once displayed, doth fall that very hour."

Viola (who knows all too well the truth of Orsino's statements) mournfully agrees, and a moment later Feste is brought in by Curio to sing a sad song of unrequited love called "Come away, come away death," which lyrically reinforces the melancholy tone of this scene.

The song deals with a lover who is "slain" by the failure of a "fair cruel maid" to respond to his amorous advances. Self-pityingly, relishing the tragedy of his love-death (much as Orsino relishes his own love-sickness), the lover asks that no flowers be strewn on his coffin, and that he be buried in an unmarked grave, since otherwise all the other "sad true lovers" in the world would breathe "a thousand sighs" over the spot.

After Feste has finished his song, been paid for his trouble and dismissed, Orsino, inspired by the music to new heights of passion, orders Viola to once more return to Olivia and once more plead his suit. Viola should tell her, he says, that he doesn't care about her lands or fortune, but only about herself-her beauty and her soul. When Viola points out to him that Olivia has already rejected him in no uncertain terms, Orsino responds that he "cannot be so answered." But you must, replies Viola, and she goes on to ask him what he thinks would happen if "some lady, as perhaps there is" (and we know there is-namely, herself) should love him as much as he loves Olivia. Since his heart is already engaged, he wouldn't be able to love her and would tell her so. Wouldn't she then, Viola inquires, have to take no for an answer, just as he must from Olivia?

Scornfully - and rather egotistically - Orsino replies that no mere woman could love as profoundly, passionately, and permanently as he does. A woman's heart isn't big enough for such a grand passion, he asserts extravagantly, and besides, "they lack retention:" that is, they're fickle. But he's contradicting himself, because just a few minutes before he'd told Viola that men are less constant than women.

Comment

In this tantalizing exchange-tantalizing because Viola hovers so close to a final revelation of her secret, and Orsino, not knowing that secret, makes such a fool of himself-Orsino shows once more how egotistical and melodramatic he can be, since it is he and not Viola who, by the end of play, will have completely abandoned his one great "true love," Olivia, for another mistress-Viola. Viola, on the other hand, shows how dangerously close she is to blurting out the truth about herself to her beloved Duke, how near the surface and nearly out of control her emotions are, and how sadly frustrated she is in her present position.

She responds to Orsino's charges about women by declaring, in a famous passage, that "they are as true of heart as we." "My father had a daughter loved a man," she tells us, "as it might be, perhaps, were I a woman/I should your lordship."

Comment

Viola is speaking, of course, of herself, though Orsino doesn't know it - and in this speech she's coming as close as she dares to an outright confession of her love for him.

Curious, Orsino asks about the fate of this unfortunate "sister" of "Cesario's." Viola replies that it's "a blank" - since the young lady never told her love, but pined away, concealing her true feelings, and "with a green and yellow melancholy" (a melancholy compounded of jealousy - obviously for Olivia - and hope), "she sat like Patience on a monument" (like a statue of Patience), "smiling at grief."

Comment

Here we have Viola's real attitude toward the difficulties of her situation. Shaken by the inner anguish of unrequited love, she doesn't even have the consolation of confessing her feelings, except thus, indirectly, and she must at all times maintain an artificial pose-like a statue-of gaiety and good cheer which she doesn't truly feel. Though Viola is a much less extravagant and melodramatic person than either Olivia or Orsino, and though she does possess to an unusual degree for a girl her age a practical and witty temperament, she's probably capable at heart (as we can see from this speech) of as deep a passion as the other two. Perhaps she even feels things more deeply.

Still intrigued - and still trying to prove the male's greater vulnerability to unrequited love - Orsino asks Viola if her "sister" died of her love. "I am all the daughters of my father's house,/ And all the brothers too, and yet I know not," the little page replies mysteriously - and then abruptly takes her leave of the Duke, departing once again for Olivia's house with a jewel from him and the message that his love will not be denied.

SUMMARY

In this beautifully balanced and musical scene we learn:

1. The extent of Viola's romantic frustration by the male disguise which keeps her from her true love, Orsino. Like the other two serious characters, Orsino and Olivia, Viola is doomed to grow increasingly melancholy (with, as she says, "a green and yellow melancholy") from the pangs of this unrequited love, before the play is over.

2. Music again is an important element of the scene. Viola's melancholy - and Orsino's more affected melancholy-are reinforced and emphasized by the

>   strains of the sad song of unrequited love which Feste sings for them.
>
> 3. We have here another opportunity to observe the Duke in the throes of his melancholy love-sickness, and compared to Viola's more sincere and less pretentious, passion, we see that his is - as we suspected before - more a series of empty and self-aggrandizing gestures than a true love.
>
> 4. The plot is furthered by the fact that Orsino once more dispatches Viola with a love-message from him to Olivia - though obviously against her own wishes, and in the face of her advice to him that the case is hopeless.
>
> 5. Serious, poignant, and lyrical in tone, this scene provides a quietly romantic contrast to the noisily comic scenes-act 2, scene 3, and act 2, scene 5-which flank it.

ACT 2: SCENE 5

This scene transports us to Olivia's garden, where Sir Toby, Sir Andrew, and another servant by the name of Fabian are preparing to conceal themselves in order to observe Malvolio's reaction to the trick Maria is going to play on him. As they gleefully anticipate the wonderful sport at hand, Maria rushes in and tells them quickly to conceal themselves behind the "boxtree" (a large kind of ornamental hedge much used by Elizabethan gardeners). Then, laughing and excitedly predicting the success of her scheme for mockery, she tosses a letter down on the garden path where Malvolio, who's been strolling and preening himself nearby, is sure to find it.

A moment later, the unlucky steward himself enters, deep in thought, which he expresses aloud in a hilarious soliloquy punctuated by bursts of outraged commentary from Toby, Andrew, and Fabian.

Comment

Nowhere else in *Twelfth Night* and hardly anywhere else in Shakespeare is the **convention** of the soliloquy used to greater comic advantage than in this scene. It may be hard for an audience, accustomed to the more realistic customs of contemporary theatre and movies, to understand how Malvolio can be thinking aloud in quite this way and still be so easily heard by the other characters onstage - without himself hearing their remarks about his thoughts - but it is an essential point to grasp here. Malvolio's speech is a soliloquy - thoughts spoken out loud-which Toby, Andrew, and Fabian are able, through the magic of the stage, to overhear. Their comments, on the other hand, are asides to the audience-as well as conversation among themselves - which Malvolio, supposedly deep in his own thoughts, is unable to overhear.

As he strolls by the boxtree, along the garden path, Malvolio is heard speculating that "tis but fortune, all is fortune." And about what subject does he have this great thought? Why - miraculously (Maria obviously understands the arrogant steward to a fare-thee-well) - none other than his mistress Olivia's fancied preference for him. For as the shrewd servingwoman had intuitively known, Malvolio has already, without the aid as yet of the letter, been led by his egotism to imagine that, were he not a member of a lower class, he - and not Orsino, Andrew, or "Cesario" - would be just the man for Olivia.

Comment

Olivia is the romantic center of the plot, just as Malvolio is (to a lesser degree) the comic center. Almost all the major male characters in the play, as well as Viola (with the exception, of course, of her cousin Toby, and the fool) at one time or another and in one way or another are romantically involved with her. Orsino and Andrew court her, Malvolio has designs on her, she herself has designs on "Cesario," and in the end Sebastian marries her.

Speculating thus about his innate suitability as a husband for Olivia, Malvolio walks slowly along. He even indulges in a wild daydream (related out loud, of course) about how, after being married for three months to Olivia and sitting in state, he'd call for "his" cousin Toby in order to chastise him for his wild behavior, as well as for the foolish company he keeps, meaning Andrew. The reactions these remarks draw from Toby and Andrew are furious indeed, and it takes all of Fabian's energy to restrain the two-especially Toby-from leaping out of their hiding place and setting on Malvolio at once.

In another moment, however, Malvolio's fantasy is interrupted. Catching sight of the letter on the path, he picks it up, curious, and begins to read it. He at once identifies the writing as "my lady's hand" - and goes on quickly, with mounting excitement, to examine the text of the letter. Maria has done her work well, as the well-concealed plotters remark, and the whole letter is designed to intrigue a mind like Malvolio's. It begins with a rhymed riddle: "Jove knows I love./ But who?/ lips do not move./ No man must know ... I may command where I adore,/ But silence, like a Lucrece knife,/ With bloodless stroke my heart doth gore./ M, O, A, I, doth sway my life."

The arrogant steward quickly interprets this obscure utterance as referring on almost every point to himself. After all, Olivia may command him, she is his lady, and all four letters mentioned are in his name. There are, of course, some obstacles: for instance, the letters are out of their proper order. But "to crush this a little," he comments, "it would bow to me" (with a little forcing, in other words, it seems to work better with him than with anyone else).

Jubilantly, he goes on to read the text of the letter, which certainly seems to be addressed to him. Written in a hilarious **parody** of his own efficiently pompous style (e.g. "Let thy tongue tang arguments of state, put thyself into the trick of singularity ..."), this prose passage advises the reader that he should not be "afraid of greatness. Some are born great, some achieve greatness, and some [obviously Malvolio] have greatness thrust upon 'em [by the favor of a great-highly placed-person like Olivia]." The letter writer then goes on to tell him in what specific ways he can show himself to be suited to this greatness which is about to descend on him. He should "be opposite with a kindsman" (Toby), "surly with servants," wear yellow-stockings, go cross-gartered, and continually smile in the presence of his lady.

Malvolio is being advised, in other words, to make a fool of himself. Yellow stockings and cross-gartering are modes of dress more suitable to servants and jesters than to Puritanical stewards; furthermore, as Maria later informs us, Olivia detests the color yellow. As for being surly with servants and smiling to Olivia - the surliness will only antagonize the servants, and the smiles will be most unwelcome in Olivia's predominantly melancholy mood.

Comment

Malvolio's willingness to believe that all these mad actions will advance him in his lady's affections is just another sign of the extent to which his egotistical arrogance will allow him to deceive himself about the reality of a situation. Furthermore, his most un-Puritanical daydreams of luxury and readiness to cast off his Puritan attire for more frivolous styles show that, as Maria had noticed, even his Puritanism is hypocritical, an affectation maintained in the service of his self-centered ambitiousness.

At any rate, gullibly believing every word of the false letter, Malvolio is soon beside himself with joy. Resolving to be "strange stout haughty, in yellow stockings and cross-gartered, he exits crying "Jove, I thank thee. I will smile, I will do everything that thou wilt have me." From his point of view, he is already successful.

The plotters, left alone onstage, emerge from behind the boxtree convulsed with merriment. Significantly enough, in view of later developments, Toby exclaims that "I could marry this wench for this device," and when Maria herself appears, flushed with pride in her own cleverness, all three vie with each other to congratulate her. She asks if the trick has really worked, and when they assure her that it most certainly has, she tells them to be sure to see how Malvolio behaves in his next interview with Olivia. In his yellow stockings and cross-gartered, a color and a style the lady can't stand, he's sure to be the very opposite of a hit. As for his smiling, with the melancholy Olivia, it's sure to "turn him into a notable contempt." And "if you will see it, follow me," cries the high-spirited Maria-at which all three rush off in a burst of excitement to gather the fruits of their sport.

SUMMARY

This scene doesn't advance the romantic plot at all, but it is a central scene in the unfolding of the comic plot.

1. In it, Malvolio comes upon the letter which Maria has tricked him into believing was written by Olivia. His hilariously solemn reaction to its content, as well as his egotistical willingness to believe that the noble Olivia could ever possibly be attracted to an arrogant, foolish steward like himself make for a revealing and comic episode.

2. The letter itself, with its wonderfully funny instructions to the reader and its clever **parody** of Malvolio's own style, is a testament to Maria's superior wit and cunning. This is instantly recognized by Sir Toby, who vows that he could marry her for her cleverness-a statement which no one takes very seriously at the time, but on which he ultimately makes good.

3. The servant Fabian is introduced for the first time in this scene. Though he doesn't have a very important part to play, he's a typical, sly, merrymaking Elizabethan servant, the sort of character with whom higher-born aristocrats like Toby and Andrew like to spend their time, and the exact opposite of an ambitious prig like Malvolio.

4. Toby and Andrew act, respectively, as wild and as silly as ever.

TWELFTH NIGHT

TEXTUAL ANALYSIS

ACT 3

ACT 3: SCENE 1

As this scene begins, we are still in Olivia's garden. Viola - apparently in the midst of executing the commission to once more woo Olivia on which Orsino sent her at the end of act 2, scene 4 - enters from one direction and encounters Feste who, carrying a tabor (a small drum), is approaching the house from another direction. She greets him pleasantly and they indulge in a bit of casual banter in order to pass the time more merrily. For instance, when Viola asks Feste if he lives by his tabor - that is, lives on the proceeds of his performances on the tabor - he replies teasingly that he lives by the church, "for I do live at my house, and my house doth stand by [near] the church."

Later, when she asks him if he's the Lady Olivia's fool, which he is, he denies it, remarking that "the Lady Olivia has no folly. She will keep no fool, sir, til she be married," - and he goes on to show how husbands are like fools. Viola, referring to act 2, scene

4, in which Feste had sung "Come away, death" at the Duke's palace, comments that she had seen him at Orsino's - and Feste answers punningly that "Foolery, sir, does walk about the orb like the sun. It shines everywhere."

Comment

In this remark, as throughout this dialogue, the words "fool" and "foolery" are used in a double-sense, to refer both to foolishness (like Andrew's feeble-mindedness or even Orsino's and Olivia's love-struck silliness) and clowning (like Feste's professional jesting).

Viola, pleased with the fool's ready wit, tosses him a coin, and when Feste slyly asks for another ("Would not a pair of these have bred, sir?"), she comments appreciatively on his clever style of begging, and rewards him with another. A moment later he exits and she's left alone briefly to speculate on the nature of such "wise" foolery as Feste's. It is, she decides, "a practice/ As full of labor as a wise man's art," for though the fool's remarks seem light-hearted and spontaneous enough, they're almost always ingeniously constructed to express several ideas at once, and they're always carefully chosen to accord as well as possible with the mood and personality of the audience toward which they're directed.

As she finishes her soliloquy, Sir Toby and Sir Andrew enter, and the three exchange courtly greetings. Andrew, especially, trying to show off his reputed facility with languages, addresses Viola in French. But before their witty banter can develop into more than a brief exchange, Olivia enters, accompanied by Maria. Viola salutes her with extravagant courtesy, exclaiming "Most excellent, accomplished lady, the heavens rain odors on you!" Andrew, impressed, remarks to Toby that "that youth's a rare courtier," and when Viola continues elaborately "My matter hath no voice, lady, but to your own most pregnant (receptive) and vouchsafed (condescending) ear," the foolish knight is overwhelmed by the dazzling elegance of her language. Olivia, of course, is also impressed by "Cesario" (she's been pining away with love of "him" for the last few days), and so she quickly dismisses Toby, Andrew, and Maria in order to hear the "youth's" message.

As soon as the two are left alone, Olivia begins eagerly to "make up" to Viola. First, she asks her name - a simple fact which she hasn't been able yet to ascertain. When Viola replies, "Cesario is your servant's name, fair princess," the unhappy lady complains that "Cesario" is unfortunately not her servant, but Orsino's. Viola answers courteously that, since Orsino is Olivia's servant, his servant must need be her servant too. Olivia responds impatiently that she really doesn't want to think about Orsino and, when Viola reminds her that she has only come on his behalf, she impetuously - unable to contain her passionate feelings for "Cesario" any longer - begs the "youth" to "undertake another suit" - his own.

Viola tries to interrupt, but before she can stop her, the lovestruck Countess rushes headlong into a full declaration of her love. She confesses her motives in sending the ring to Cesario, and admits that the "youth" might well have been justified in harshly interpreting the "shameful cunning" of her act. But, she explains, she couldn't help herself. Now her feelings must be obvious to Cesario - and she wonders what "his" reaction to them is. Viola answers frankly, and briefly, that she pities her - and Olivia hopefully remarks that at least pity is a step toward love. But Viola rudely shatters this illusion, commenting that "very oft we pity enemies."

> **Comment**

Viola is being absolutely honest with Olivia, because though she does, in fact, pity the love-sick Countess as the victim of a truly unfortunate misunderstanding, she basically regards her as an enemy on account of Orsino's love for her.

Shattered by Viola's forceful rejection of her romantic advances, Olivia tries to pull herself together, blaming the "youth's" attitude on "his" pride. When she hears a clock striking in the distance, she exclaims distractedly that she realizes she's wasting time, and "be not afraid, good youth, I will not have you." "But still, she adds, when "Cesario" is old enough to wed, his wife is "like to reap a proper man." With this, she dismisses "him" and Viola, relieved, prepares to depart, first asking politely if Olivia has any messages for Orsino.

Olivia, however, though she has made a valiant effort to tear herself away from Cesario, has still not gotten her feelings entirely under control, and she begs Viola to tell her, before leaving, "what thou think'st of me." Viola replies ambiguously "that you do think you are not what you are" - that is, that in loving Cesario and rejecting Orsino, you estimate yourself wrongly.

> **Comment**

There's an element of social as well as emotional tension in this exchange, because, though Viola is by birth as well-placed as Olivia, her present position is that of a servant. Therefore, Olivia imagines that Viola is rejecting her out of pride and because of her relative poverty, and Viola finds it convenient to perpetuate the idea, implying that a proper valuation of her social position should lead Olivia to accept Orsino-her social equal - and stop running after his servant, Cesario-her inferior. The line "that you do think you are not what you are" also implies that Olivia is mistaken in her self-judgment because she thinks she's in love with a man, when in reality she's in love with a woman.

Olivia responds excitedly that the same might apply to Viola - that is, that in rejecting Olivia's advances out of false pride, Viola is undervaluing herself too. To this, Viola replies, "then think you right. I am not what I am" - a remark which is not only mysterious, but also true, since the young messenger is not a man, as she appears, but a woman. "I would you were as I would have you be" - that is, I wish you'd let yourself love me, and stop being so proud - answers Olivia. This annoys Viola, who asks if it would be better than she now is - "I wish it might, for now I am your fool."

Surprisingly, this angry remark only melts the passionate Olivia into a deeper romantic ecstasy. "Oh what a deal of scorn looks beautiful/In the contempt and anger of his lip!" she swoons, and launches into a wild declaration of love, more forthright and emphatic than any yet. By "the roses of the spring/ By maidhood, honor, truth and everything," she swears extravagantly, her love for Cesario is so intense that despite all this "youth's" scornful pride, she can't hide her feelings. Therefore she begs "him" at least not to reject her because she, the woman, who should be passive, is actively doing the wooing-but rather, to accept her gift of love freely, since love sought is good, but given unsought is better."

Now Viola is carried away by her feelings too. She sympathizes with the unhappy Olivia, but, of course, she cannot return her love. More than anything she wishes that she could tell this love-lorn Countess the whole truth of the matter, but since she can't do that, at least she can assure her with all the earnestness and solemnity she can summon up, that "no woman" will ever be mistress of her heart "save I alone." She swears this "by innocence" and "by my youth" - and thus swearing bids Olivia emphatically adieu (not au revoir). "Nevermore," she declares, will I my master's tears to you deplore."

But Olivia, still hopeful despite this clear-cut rejection, begs Cesario to "come again, for thou perhaps mayst move/ That heart which now abhors to like his (Orsino's) love" - a possibility which both know is as remote as is the likelihood of Viola's ever returning Olivia's love. And on this note the two depart, in different directions - Olivia to closet herself again with in her house, distractedly mourning her brother and pining after the scornful Cesario, and Viola to return, in frustration, to Orsino's palace, where she must herself endure the pangs of unrequited love.

SUMMARY

This varied and carefully constructed scene is one of the dramatic high-spots of the play.

1. Most important, Olivia declares her love for Cesario in it, and is rejected outright by the disguised Viola, who knows, of course, as Olivia doesn't, the impossibility of the situation. The frustration of both characters mounts throughout their passionate lyrical confrontation, and the emotional tension between them has become almost unbearable by the time they leave the stage.

    (a) Olivia is frustrated because she believes that Cesario will not let "himself" love her on account of false pride. She thinks that "he" is sensitive about being her social inferior, and also that "he" doesn't approve of the woman being the aggressor in a romantic situation.

(b) Viola is frustrated because she feels sorry for Olivia, and would like to tell her the truth about her identity, but she doesn't dare. Furthermore, she regards Olivia as her rival for the affections of Orsino and finds it hard to listen to such a declaration of love from a kind of "enemy."

2. As if to prepare the way gently for its dramatic **climax** - and to provide a comic contrast with the seriousness of its conclusion - the scene opens with a few minutes of witty banter between Feste, the fool, and Viola. This gives us another view of Feste's cleverness, as well as, more significantly, another chance to assess Viola's practical wit and wisdom. She's witty in her ready, good-humored replies to the jester's barbed remarks, and she's wise in her careful judgment of the true value of "foolery" such as his. In this she shows herself to be made of the same aristocratic stuff as Olivia, who, in act 1, scene 5, defended the clown's worth to the scornful and uncomprehending Malvolio.

3. Viola also shows the range of her talents in her courtly address of Olivia when that lady and Maria first enter the garden in the presence of Toby and Andrew. Andrew, for one, is to impressed by Viola's courtly skill, and by Olivia's favorable reception of the "youth" (a reception such as he has never been accorded) that, as we shall see in the next scene,

he rather gets his blood up. The jealousy of Viola which inspires his upcoming challenge was skillfully motivated by Shakespeare in just about twenty lines in this scene.

ACT 3: SCENE 2

This scene returns us to the interior of Olivia's house, where Sir Andrew appears with Sir Toby and Fabian. The foolish knight is vehemently expressing his determination to leave at once for home. When Toby and Faby ask him his reason, he bitterly complains that Olivia has bestowed more favors on "the count's servingman [Cesario] than ever she bestowed on me." He's referring to the scene which just occurred in the garden in which Olivia had peremptorily dismissed Toby, Maria and himself from her presence in order to be alone with Viola.

Comment

As we saw, Andrew's jealousy was roused in act 3, scene 1 not only by Olivia's kindness to Cesario, but also by Viola's skill in handling the language and the style of the court, with which he, Andrew, is really unfamiliar. For though he is a knight, the weak-minded Andrew is also essentially a country bumpkin, a stranger to the elegant world of the Illyrian court, the high society in which characters like Orsino, Olivia, and Viola move with such ease and assurance.

Sir Toby and Fabian cleverly make fun of Andrew's complaints by arguing that Olivia had deliberately shown favor to Cesario in front of Andrew in order to "awake" his "dormouse valor" and try his mettle. In other words, they try to make the gullible knight believe that Olivia is really interested in him and wants to make him jealous by flirting with Cesario. What Andrew ought to have done, they maintain, is shown up the Count's "man" by outshining him on the spot with even more witty and more courtly language than "he" could produce.

Comment

Fabian, in particular, amuses himself and Toby by delivering this opinion to Andrew in the most elaborate metaphorical language (e.g. "The double gilt of this opportunity you have let time wash off...") which only mystifies and upsets the poor knight still more.

Finally, Toby suggests that since he didn't take the opportunity-as he should have-to put Cesario down in Olivia's presence by outdoing "his" wit, the only alternative left Andrew is to challenge the insolent "youth" to a duel. When Fabian agrees, Andrew readily enough sets out to compose an angry letter to Cesario. Toby, egging him on still further, urges him to "write it in a martial hand" and make it as ferocious as possible.

After Andrew has hurried off to carry out Toby's instructions, Fabian and Toby delightedly discuss the sport that will soon be at hand. Fabian remarks that Andrew is a "dear manikin" to Toby - that is, a wonderful puppet for the jolly knight to amuse himself with - and Toby replies punningly that he (Toby) has been "dear" (expensive) to Andrew to the tune of some two thousand ducats. The two agree that Andrew's challenge to Cesario ought to provide some "rare" amusement - and they agree further that the duel itself should be pretty funny since Cesario, too, "bears in his visage no great presage of cruelty" - an understatement if ever there was one, since Viola, as a gently-reared young girl, can hardly dissemble masculinity to the extent of fighting a duel.

Suddenly, however, as the two pleasure-lovers are rapt in contemplation of the hilarious scene to come, Maria enters, convulsed with merriment, with news of further sport. Amid gales of laughter, she notifies them that Malvolio has carried out all the orders in the letter and is even now approaching his mistress in his mad new fashion-smiling, yellow-stockinged, and cross-gartered. "I know my lady will strike him," Maria giggles, and "If she do, he'll smile and take't for a great favor." Overjoyed at the success of their scheme, the three rush off to watch the fun.

SUMMARY

1. This scene, which is purely comic, effectively relieves the highly charged romantic tension which had built up by the end of act 3, scene

2. Andrew's ludicrous jealousy of Viola (which we saw developing in the previous scene) is the comic center of this scene.

   (a) It sheds further light on Andrew's weak, egotistical character, and on Toby's exploitation of it. This exploitation, like Toby's financial manipulation of Andrew, shows the fat knight's basic selfishness. Fabian's willingness to go along with the gag is also typical of his personality.

   (b) The challenge which Toby and Fabian induce Andrew to write leads directly to the hilarious duel between Viola and Andrew in act 3, scene 4, a duel whose repercussions involve not only these two characters but also Sebastian and Antonio, indirectly bringing about the **denouement** of the

> play, in which Olivia marries Sebastian. Thus the comic and the romantic plots begin to merge at this point.
>
> 3. We learn that the scheme to "gull" Malvolio has been successful, and we're prepared to witness a scene (coming up soon) in which he will make a perfect fool of himself.

ACT 3: SCENE 3

Sebastian and Antonio have just met on an Illyrian street, and Sebastian who - as we recall from act 2, scene 1 - had begged Antonio not to follow him to Illyria, is greeting his friend fondly. He hadn't wanted him to come, he explains, but he's glad to see him now that he's here. Antonio assures Sebastian of his love and loyalty. Despite the danger of being in such hostile territory, he could hardly stay behind, he declares, knowing that Sebastian was "unguarded and unfriended" here, especially since his own experiences with the Illyrians have always been so unpleasant. Sebastian once again thanks him for his kindness and concern, and then, with all the zeal of a young tourist - forgetting his recent troubles - he asks what there is to do in this town, and suggests that the two of them set out to see whatever sights there may be. Antonio tries to put him off, suggesting that they take lodgings first, but Sebastian insists that he's not tired and enthusiastically repeats his suggestion that they do the town.

Finally Antonio is forced to reluctantly admit that he's really in danger on these streets, since "once in a sea fight" he'd inflicted much damage on Orsino's navy, and the Illyrians would be only too eager to revenge themselves on him if they could take him captive. Sebastian remarks that he must certainly have killed a lot of Illyrians to have aroused such hostility, but Antonio replies that the business was more in the nature of a hold-up-not bloody, but costly to the Illyrians in terms of goods and cash. He himself, he claims, performed with the utmost distinction in this battle (and a full-fledged battle it apparently was, between Antonio's unnamed native city and Illyria) and for this reason Orsino's men are especially anxious to lay their hands on him. At this, Sebastian agrees that Antonio should definitely not "walk too open," and they decide to meet at the Elephant, an inn in "the south suburbs" well known to Antonio. The latter is to go there and order dinner while Sebastian tours the town at his leisure.

Comment

There was a famous London inn on the south side of the Thames, known as the Elephant in Shakespeare's day-further evidence, if any was needed, that the playwright was thinking more in terms of England and Englishmen than of Illyria and Illyrians when he wrote *Twelfth Night*. The inn still exists, but is now called the Elephant and Castle.

Finally, before taking leave of Sebastian, Antonio comments that he knows his friend doesn't have much money, and generously offers him his purse, in case he should see any little things he'd like to buy himself while he's wandering about the town. Sebastian gratefully accepts, and the two go off in different directions, agreeing to meet in an hour at the Elephant.

SUMMARY

1. We learn from this brief scene that Sebastian and Antonio have finally arrived in Illyria. The stage is thus set for the dramatic complications of mistaken

identity which will bring the play to its happy conclusion.

2. We learn more about Antonio from

   (a) the fact that he loves Sebastian enough to be willing to follow him into such dangerous territory - and from

   (b) the story that he tells about the offense (evidently a kind of piracy) which he committed against the Illyrians.

   (c) Antonio's generous loan of his purse to Sebastian will be important to the plot later on, when he mistakes Viola for her brother and demands its return.

3. Sebastian's exuberant interest in seeing the sights of the town shows that, like Viola, he's of a practical, optimistic turn of mind, more in love with life than inclined to prolong his "grief" for the loss of a sister.

ACT 3: SCENE 4

We once more find ourselves in Olivia's garden, where Olivia herself, still absorbed in romantic thoughts of Cesario, enters with Maria. More to herself than to her solicitous servingwoman, she mentions rather agitatedly that she's sent for the "youth" and "he's" agreed to come. "How shall I feast him?" she wonders, "What bestow of (on) him?" Looking around, she asks Malvolio's whereabouts. Perhaps he can advise her because he is so "sad" and "civil" (serious).

Comment

By now-on the advice of the letter - the ambitious steward (who was agreeable enough to Olivia in his usual solemnfaced manner) is the very opposite of "sad and civil".

Maria assures Olivia, as demurely as she can - choking back her laughter - that Malvolio is coming, but "in very strange manner." In fact, his manner is so strange that the little attendant declares he must be "possessed," that is, mad. Concerned, Olivia asks why. "Does he rave?" Maria replies gravely that "he does nothing but smile" - and yet Olivia would probably be better off with some kind of guard about her, because the man is clearly crazy. At this, Olivia demands that Maria call him hither, for "I am as mad as he,/ If sad and merry madness equal be."

Comment

This is a perceptive remark of Olivia's, for though she's not madly deluded in the way Malvolio s, she recognizes that her extravagant melancholy is as unnatural and foreign to her own healthy temperament as Malvolio's crazed "merriness" is unnatural and mad for his temperament.

Maria leaves to fetch Malvolio and re-enters a moment later with the crazily costumed steward. He's followed the instructions of his mysterious correspondent to the letter, and he's wearing bright yellow stockings with garters wrapped around them in a zig-zag pattern (cross-garters). He greets Olivia with a cheery "Sweet lady, ho ho." There ensues a long comical exchange between the two, during which Malvolio misinterprets every one of Olivia's remarks in terms of the letter he's purportedly received from her.

When she tells him that she sent for him because she was feeling sad, for instance, he replies that he supposes he could be sad too, (since his garters are so uncomfortably tight, but continues with a meaningful leer that "if it please the eye of one" it's all right with him. Again, when she asks if he wants to go to bed (because he's sick) he gleefully misunderstands her solicitude as an invitation to him and exclaims "Aye, sweetheart, and I'll come to thee." Olivia is appalled by this behavior, and she's certainly not enlightened when he answers her repeated questions ("Why dost thou smile and kiss thy hand so oft?" etc.) with knowing winks and references to the letter. Finally, when she's at her wit's end, a servant enters to inform her that Cesario has reluctantly obeyed her summons and is waiting for her in the house. With a few distracted words to Maria - "Let this fellow be looked to . . . Let some of my people have a special care of him" - she rushes off to see Viola, but not without first commending the unfortunate Malvolio to the special care of her cousin Toby.

Comment

Malvolio has certainly fallen into the worst hands possible, since we can be sure Toby and company will make the most they can of his foolish behavior. Olivia's reaction to his "madness," however, has been commendably sympathetic. Indeed, it's hard to think of her as anything but a basically kind and goodhearted person (though Viola calls her "proud") on the basis of her treatment of Malvolio, Toby, and the other members of her household.

Alone onstage for a moment, Malvolio soliloquizes jubilantly on the fancied success of his venture. He's so self-deluded and egotistical that he hasn't noticed anything in the least strange about Olivia's response to his amorous advances. On the contrary, he imagines he's a great romantic hit with her. The fact that she's called for Toby to take care of him, for example, strikes him as concurring "directly with the letter." He imagines she's deliberately sent Toby so he can be "stubborn to him," as the letter directed. Excitedly, he repeats whole passages of the letter (which he evidently knows by heart by now) and exclaims that "Nothing that can be can come between me and the full prospect of my hopes."

Comment

Though Malvolio's "mad" behavior has been, in fact, deliberately induced by Maria's crafty scheming, there is nonetheless something really mad about the arrogant steward. He's mad - not because he wears yellow stockings and goes cross-gartered (the letter instructed him to do those things) - but rather because he has so allowed his egotism and his ambition to run away with him that by now he's completely out of touch with reality. He doesn't even notice that Olivia's reaction to his leering advances is compassionate, rather than passionate, and the unlikelihood of her ever addressing such a love message to him in the first place has never even occurred to him.

Now Maria returns with Toby and Fabian (we saw her actually informing them of their plot's success at the very end of act 3, scene 2). Toby is playing his part well, loudly resolving that even if Malvolio is "possessed" by "all the devils of Hell," he will speak to him. Fabian, as usual, readily goes along with the joke, inquiring of Malvolio in noisily sympathetic tones "How is't with you man?" Malvolio scornfully rejects the trio as, incidentally, the letter had instructed him to. He imagines this is all meant as a test of his mettle on Olivia's part. But they persist in their sport. "Lo, how hollow the fiend speaks within him,"

Maria cries ominously, and all three melodramatically urge the contemptuous steward to "defy the devil."

By now Malvolio is getting pretty annoyed-but he endures their behavior grimly, convinced that Olivia is on his side. When Toby actually talks babytalk to him, asking insolently "How dost thou chuck?" (as one would humor a sick person) he makes no response but an indignant "Sir!" and when Maria suggests that he say his prayers, he withers her (or so he thinks) with a contemptuous "My prayers, minx!" Finally, however, their remarks are too much for him, and he angrily tells them to go hang themselves, exiting with the scornful statement that they are "idle, shallow things" and he, Malvolio, is not of their "element."

The minute Malvolio is gone, Toby, Fabian, and Maria roar with laughter at the wonderful sport they've had with him. Fabian even comments that the whole scheme would be thought "improbable" if it were seen on the stage-a reference such as Shakespeare was fond of making to the fact that the whole scheme is being seen on the stage. But when Maria suggests that they "pursue" the unfortunate steward further, lest he come to his senses too soon, the wily Fabian expresses the fear that they may "make him mad indeed." Toby and Maria, however, feel no such misgivings about the prospect, and they agree to "have him in a dark room and bound" before they give up their revenge. When they finally do decide to have mercy on him, Toby flatteringly tells Maria, "we will...crown thee for a finder of madmen."

But before they can discuss their plans for Malvolio's future any more, Sir Andrew Aguecheek appears, flushed and emboldened with his own egotism, carrying the challenge he's just written to Cesario. "I warrant there's salt and pepper in it," he says, handing it to Toby to read.

In its own way, Andrew's letter to Cesario is as much of a masterpiece as Maria's letter to Malvolio-only in this case it's brilliant as a self-parody, not a **burlesque** of another's style, and notable for its witlessness rather than its wit. Among other things, the "valiant" Andrew informs Cesario that "whatsoever thou art, thou art a scurvy fellow," and goes on to add, however, that Cesario shouldn't wonder at this abuse for he, Andrew, will give him no reason for it. The letter then continues, senselessly, "thou comest to the Lady Olivia, and in my sight she uses thee kindly, but thou liest in thy throat" - a bitter and, in this case, irrational insult, since it has nothing to do with anything else that's been mentioned. Toby and Fabian comment approvingly on all this, evidently having as much fun with the stupidly egotistical Andrew as they did with the madly egotistical Malvolio. Next, the letter threatens that Andrew will "waylay" Cesario on his way home, but warns that if Cesario kills Andrew he'll be doing it "like a rogue and a villain." "Still you keep on the windy [safe> side of the law," remarks Fabian in mock appreciation of Andrew's cleverness. Finally, the letter concludes, feebly, "Fare thee well, and God have mercy upon one of our souls! He may have mercy upon mine, but my hope is better, and so look to thyself. Thy friend, as thou usest him, and thy sworn enemy. Andrew Aguecheek.

Maria, Toby and Fabian join to compliment the foolish knight on his great work and Toby, as usual, leads his protégé on to even greater heights of silliness, encouraging him to await Cesario in the orchard and when the unfortunate "youth" appears, to draw his sword at once and "swear horrible." Andrew proudly assures his friends that he's an expert at swearing, and rushes off in a wild fit of what he thinks is ferocity to carry out his mission.

After he's left, Toby tells Maria and Fabian that he certainly doesn't plan to deliver Andrew's idiotic letter to Cesario, since any well-brought-up young man could tell from such a foolish production that its writer is nothing more than a "clodpole" (block-head). He will rather, he declares, deliver the challenge himself, in person, and describe the faint-hearted Aguecheek's courage, strength and fury in such glowing terms that the very young and mild-mannered Cesario will be terrified of him and "they will kill one another by the look, like cockatrices." (A cockatrice was a mythical serpent, able to kill by its mere look).

At just this moment Viola herself enters, with Olivia. The two are still deep in conversation and so Toby, Fabian, and Maria leave to await their farewell. Olivia, miserable, is complaining that Cesario has "a heart of stone" and that she knows she shouldn't persist in her romantic advances to "him" but she can't help herself. Viola replies loyally that her "master's grief" is every bit as intense as the passion Olivia feels-but Olivia ignores this and, offering Viola-Cesario a jewel with her picture in it as a lovetoken, begs "him" to return again tomorrow. But when she asks Cesario if there's anything else she can give "him" within reason, Viola replies again, adamantly, "your true love for my master." Olivia answers that this request is unreasonable, since she's already given her love to Cesario - and so the two ruefully take their leave, Olivia once again begging Viola to return, and Viola, as courteously as possible under the circumstances bidding her goodbye.

As soon as Olivia is gone, Toby and Fabian re-enter and accost Viola, who is herself about to leave the garden. Toby immediately informs her of the challenge Andrew has made to her, and then goes on to terrify her with a vivid description of her "interceptor, full of despite (spite) and bloody as the hunter." Viola, even more frightened than Toby could have imagined she'd be (since he doesn't realize that she's not even a young man), assures him that there must be some mistake, since she's never done anyone any harm. But Toby insists that she must have, and "if you hold your life at any price, betake you to your guard." He then goes on to describe Andrew as a skillful knight, "a devil in private brawl," who's already killed three men in duels. When Viola tries to escape, exclaiming that she'll return to the house and get Olivia to provide her with an armed escort, since she's no fighter, Toby restrains her, declaring that her opponent's indignation is well justified in his opinion, and Viola must give him some satisfaction or else take on Toby himself.

Poor Viola, mystified and upset, begs to know what she could have done to offend so powerful a knight. Whatever it was, she didn't do it deliberately, she declares, in her most conciliatory tone. Offering to negotiate for her with her wrathful accuser, Toby leaves her alone for a moment with Fabian, who cleverly takes this opportunity to tell her that though Andrew doesn't look like very much, she's sure to find him the most "skillful, bloody and fatal opposite" that she could find in Illyria. Fabian then slyly offers to make her peace with Andrew, if he can. She gratefully accepts his offer, explaining that she's a gentle person who would rather associate with peaceful priests than bloody knights of this description.

Comment

For the second time Viola's disguise has gotten her into real trouble. First it allowed Olivia to fall in love with her mistakenly, and now it's allowed Andrew to erroneously challenge her to a duel. This second occurrence, if anything, throws her into even more of a panic than the former problem, since as a well-bred young girl she's been trained in the kind of courtesy and wit that's necessary for a diplomatic rejection of the love-struck countess, but she's never, of course, been given any practice in the lethal art of dueling.

Viola and Fabian leave the stage for a moment, presumably to try to negotiate a peace with Andrew, but a moment later Andrew himself is dragged onstage by Toby. Toby-whose capacity for mischief-making is endless - is now engaged in assuring the terrified Andrew that Cesario is himself "a very devil . . . They say he has been fencer to the Sophy [the Shah of Iran]," he declares. Poor Andrew immediately tries to escape, exclaiming "Pox on't, I'll not meddle with him," but Toby, who is looking forward to this sport, won't let him go. Frantic, Andrew offers to pacify the supposedly enraged Cesario by giving him his horse. Toby agrees to "make the motion" to the "youth" - and then slyly remarks, in an aside to the audience, that he himself will manage to keep the horse-still further evidence of his unscrupulous exploitation of his friend.

    Now Fabian and Viola re-enter, with Viola trailing as reluctantly behind Fabian as Andrew behind Toby. Though both duellers are straining away from each other, pale with fear, the two plotters-Toby and Fabian-urge them on.

Comment

When it's performed onstage, this brief encounter between Andrew and Viola is one of the funniest duels in all theater. Just as the letters written to Malvolio and by Andrew are hilarious parodies of different letter-writing styles (the mysterious riddle, the bold challenge) so the duel between Viola and Andrew is a wonderful **burlesque** of a duel, in which both opponents are so reluctant to fight that they have to be literally dragged into the proper positions by their seconds.

    Finally Viola and Andrew draw their swords and are about to have a pass at each other when-of all people-Sebastian's friend

TWELFTH NIGHT

Antonio enters, and demands that Andrew put up his sword. "If this young gentleman have done offense," he cries loyally, "I take the fault on me," and before anyone realizes what has happened, he and Toby (who is furious at this interference) are lunging at each other with a will.

Suddenly, however, a group of officers of the law appear, and the fighting immediately stops. (Duelling was illegal in Elizabethan England.) It seems, however, that the officers haven't been summoned to break up a brawl, but rather to arrest Antonio, who's been recognized-as he feared he might be-as a notorious enemy of the state. He protests that the men are mistaken, but they're adamant. "I know your favor (face) well," one of them insists. Evidently he's been on their most wanted list for quite a while. As he's being led away, Antonio turns to Viola and, thinking she's Sebastian, asks for his purse. He's sorry to have to deprive his friend of funds, he explains, but now he'll need some money himself.

Viola, uncomprehending, is dumbfounded, and doesn't answer. Antonio, again - this time with some irritation - asks for his money. Finally Viola's voice returns and she asks him "What money?" She gladly acknowledges his kindness in rescuing her from her trouble with Andrew, she says, but she doesn't know what purse he's talking about. However, because he's been so good to her, she offers to split her own small store of gold with him, since he's obviously in need. Outraged by what he thinks is Sebastian's ingratitude, Antonio begins to berate "him" for it.

Viola, still mystified, denies that he's ever done anything else special for her - and is especially upset by the charge of ingratitude, which she says she hates more than almost any other vice in a man. Antonio is almost speechless with rage, but as the officers start to hurry him off he begs to be allowed to tell his story. He just recently rescued this "youth" from "the jaws of death," he declares, and he'd thought the "boy's" charm and attractiveness worthy of much devotion. The officers, indifferent to his anguish, try again to hustle him away, but he won't be stilled. Turning to Viola, he addresses her as Sebastian, exclaiming "Thou hast, Sebastian, done good feature shame" - meaning that he'd loved Sebastian for his good looks, but that the very idea of beauty is debased by Sebastian's immoral and ungrateful denial of friendship. "Virtue is beauty, but the beauteous evil," he cries in bitter rage and disappointment, "are empty trunks, o'er flourished by the Devil" - over-elaborately carved chests, which have nothing inside. At this, "the man grows mad," one of the officers declares, and they lead him forcibly off, leaving Viola behind to ponder wonderingly on his words.

Comment

This is the first time Viola has heard her brother's name mentioned since she's been in Illyria, but to her quick mind it's immediately obvious from the fact that Antonio addressed her as Sebastian, that the unfortunate captain has probably mistaken her for him - and that, in fact, Sebastian must be at this very moment not only alive, but nearby.

Thinking it all out carefully, she remarks in a brief soliloquy that she knows her brother to be still "living in [her] glass" - that is, the image of herself which she sees daily in her mirror is also her brother's image, since she's deliberately imitated him in her dress, style and manner. If he should be alive, as she thinks he is, the supposedly cruel sea has been kind indeed, and she rushes off, completely absorbed in her joyful thoughts.

Toby, Andrew, and Fabian, left behind onstage, discuss sourly what "a very dishonest paltry boy" Cesario must be to have treated his friend (Antonio) so ungratefully. Besides, Toby and Fabian add, he's a coward. This imbues Andrew with the spirit of battle once more, and he vows to follow Cesario and beat him. Delighted at the prospect of a renewal of their sport, Toby and Fabian egg him on, and the three hurry off once again in hot pursuit of poor Viola.

SUMMARY

In this scene - the longest in the play and longer (430 lines) than all of either act 4 or 5 - the comic and romantic plots finally merge.

1. Maria's scheme to "gull" Malvolio comes to a head. To Olivia's dismay and to the delight of the conspirators (Toby, Fabian, Andrew, and Maria) Malvolio makes as big a fool of himself as the letter had told him to. His ridiculous behavior, in fact, sheds further light on the extent of his egotism, for anyone who could allow himself to be so deluded by vanity and ambition must be indeed "sick of self-love."

2. Andrew's jealousy of Viola-which was conceived in act 3, scene 2-leads him to challenge her to a duel. Like Malvolio's "madness," Andrew's behavior is also based on egotism-again, like Malvolio's, on a foolishly egotistical willingness to believe that a well-born beauty like Olivia could stoop to loving him.

    (a) In the duel, the comic and romantic plots merge. Viola, a "serious" character, has come to see Olivia on a serious errand, but the duel in which she becomes involved is one of the play's chief comic events.

(b) Her "rescue" from her "ferocious" opponent (Andrew) by Antonio further interweaves the comic and romantic elements of the plot. Antonio's strange behavior ultimately conveys to Viola the good news that her brother Sebastian is still alive. Furthermore, the fact that he so readily confuses her with her brother prepares the way for Olivia in act 4 to make a similar mistake, but one with even more resounding repercussions.

(c) Olivia herself still hasn't given up on Cesario, and the fact that it was she who summoned "him" to the scene of the duel and who aroused Andrew's rage in the first place by her favorable treatment of the Duke's "man" is further evidence that the comic and romantic strands of the plot are no longer as easy to separate as they were earlier in the action.

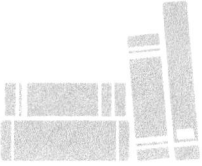

TWELFTH NIGHT

TEXTUAL ANALYSIS

ACT 4

ACT 4: SCENE 1

This scene takes place in front of Olivia's house, where Sebastian-who's been doing some casual sightseeing in the town, as he told Antonio he would-is waylaid by Feste, the fool, with a message from Olivia. Sebastian, of course, has never laid eyes on this fellow before, and so he can't understand why Feste (who naturally thinks he's Cesario) should have any business with him. Feste, amazed in his turn by Cesario's strange behavior, becomes sarcastic: "No, I do not know thee," he exclaims ironically, "nor this is not my nose neither. Nothing that is so is so." But Sebastian refuses to be intimidated by his sharpness, telling him to go "vent" his "folly somewhere else. Thou knowst not me," Feste, even more annoyed, still can't believe that Cesario doesn't know him, and asks him once more what he should tell Olivia. Sebastian, torn between amazement at this mad mistake and irritation at the fool's persistence, tosses Feste a few coins and tells him threateningly to be off or he'll be paid further in blows instead of coins.

Comment

Sebastian, of course, cannot jump to conclusions about the reason for Feste's mistake as easily as Viola could infer the reason for Antonio's, since the young man would have no reason (a) to associate the name Cesario with Viola, or (b) to imagine that this mysterious Cesario could possibly be his own sister, disguised essentially as himself. Furthermore, his angry and aggressive behavior throughout this scene - in his threats to Feste and his response to Andrew and Toby - contrasts strikingly with Viola's gentle feminine shrinking from violence. Though the two are twins, after all-with many personality traits in common - the sexual difference between them cannot be discounted.

In a moment, before Sebastian has time to make good on his threat to the fool, Andrew, Toby and Fabian enter. They'd left the garden, we recall, at the end of act 3, scene 4, in hot pursuit of Cesario. Since Fabian and Toby assured Andrew the "boy" was a coward, the foolish knight is determined to challenge "him anew, and punish" him - not only for "his" usurpation of the Countess' affections - but also for "his" ungrateful behavior to Antonio. But now, of course, they've really got the wrong man - for Sebastian is as far from being a coward as his sister is from being a warrior. Trained from birth, like any young nobleman, in fencing and fighting of all kinds, he's mystified by the challenge Andrew shouts immediately on entering, but readily enough draws his sword and lays about him with a will. "Are all the people mad?" he inquires - astonished that everyone seems to take him for someone else - even as he delivers a few well - aimed blows to the unlucky Andrew.

At this point, Toby - who's reluctant to lose his main source of income and amusement (Andrew) - intervenes in his friend's behalf, and begs "Cesario" to hold - that is, put up his sword. But Sebastian is furious mad by now, and keeps right on fighting.

In the meantime, Feste-knowing that Olivia would want to hear of such a battle royal between her kinsman and her "lover" - rushes off to tell her what's going on. Andrew, by now, has managed to get away from Sebastian, and is vowing to "have an action of battery against him, if there be any law in Illyria," though he himself started the fight in the first place, and Toby has taken on the quarrel. In fact, Toby and Sebastian are furiously duelling when Olivia, summoned by Feste, appears on the scene.

Appalled at the bloody sight she sees (and horrified that her beloved "Cesario" should have been so set on by these rascals), she orders Toby to stop fighting and immediately begins to upbraid him for his rude behavior to "Cesario," at the same time begging the really (by now) profoundly amazed Sebastian not to be offended by her cousin's barbarous manners. Andrew, Toby, and Fabian leave in chagrin, and as soon as they're gone, Olivia, still apologizing profusely for their behavior, begs Sebastian to come into the house with her and let her tell him all about the "many fruitless pranks this ruffian [Toby] hath botched up." He should forgive Toby, she says, because the fellow is always in this sort of trouble - and besides, she goes on, once more declaring her love for "Cesario," the whole thing has given her a terrible fright.

Sebastian, completely confused by this-but naturally rather pleased, as any healthy young man would be, by such unsolicited romantic attentions from such a beautiful and elegant woman- wonders whether he's awake or asleep, mad or dreaming. Finally, resigning himself to what's really become, at this point, rather a pleasant situation, he exclaims, "If it be thus to dream, still let me sleep!" Olivia-herself a little surprised to find the formerly reluctant "Cesario" now so eager for her love-asks if he "be ruled by me!" and when Sebastian replies enthusiastically 'Madam, I will," she leads him joyously off, hardly able to believe in her good fortune.

Comment

Sebastian's positive reaction to Olivia's advances, like his ready violent response to Andrew's challenge, marks another (obviously) sexual difference between him and his sister. But though much of his delight in Olivia's behavior clearly stems from his confusion and amazement at these (to him) incomprehensible romantic overtures from an attractive noblewoman, part of it probably results also from the fact that he himself almost immediately returns her passion. After all, Olivia is an exceptionally beautiful woman (as even Viola admitted) and it's not in the least surprising that Sebastian himself should have fallen in love at first sight.

SUMMARY

In this scene the comic and romantic plots are even more inextricably entangled than in the previous one.

1. Sebastian is mistaken for Cesario by Feste, Andrew, Toby, Fabian, and Olivia-as if to balance the fact that in the other scene Viola was mistaken for Sebastian by Antonio. The whole play has been leading up to these cases of mistaken identity, and as we shall see, the whole plot depends on them for its solution-for only Sebastian, a fourth member, of the right sex,

can unlock the deadlocked love-triangle of Orsino, Olivia, and Viola.

2. On the comic side, Andrew and Toby are soundly beaten by the young man-as they deserve to be-since he's as aggressively masculine as Viola is gently feminine.

3. On the romantic side, Olivia once more makes passionate advances to "Cesario," but this time she's surprised and delighted to find her feelings reciprocated-for in this respect, too, Sebastian's masculinity makes an immense difference. Besides, he's probably fallen in love at first sight with the beautiful Countess.

ACT 4: SCENE 2

This scene returns us once more to the interior of Olivia's house. Maria and the clown enter, apparently deep in some new scheme-which turns out, however, to be merely an elaboration of the old plot against Malvolio. The sly servingwoman gives the fool a priest's gown and a false beard, and instructs him to make poor Malvolio believe he's "Sir Topas," the priest. Then she rushes off to fetch Sir Toby, so he too can join in the fun.

Comment

Madness such as the conspirators are pretending Malvolio is afflicted with was commonly believed to be the result of possession by a devil. Hence priests and other religious persons were often called on to cure the sick person by exorcising the devil. The church in the Middle Ages even had a fixed and widely used ritual in which the evil spirit was ceremonially expelled.

Alone onstage for a moment, the fool makes a few witty remarks about the clergy in an aside to the audience. He says, for instance, that he will not be the first to "dissemble" in a priestly gown. Then, when Maria returns with Toby, he immediately plunges into his act as "Sir Topas." In gravely quavering tones (Feste's performance is a marvelous **burlesque** of the behavior of a silly priest) he greets the two conspirators with a few learned-sounding remarks, which are, however, no more than nonsense. Then he approaches the "prison" where Malvolio is confined.

Comment

Another common Elizabethan treatment of madmen was to chain them and lock them in dark rooms where they were fed on bread and water. It was thought that this treatment would so exasperate the demon-in-possession that he'd leave and seek a more hospitable environment. Maria considers it one of the triumphs of her scheme that it has resulted in such therapy for Malvolio, who is even now supposedly imprisoned in a bare, unlighted room in Olivia's house-usually indicated onstage by a high screen dividing the corner in which Malvolio stands from the larger area where Maria, Toby, and the clown appear. In some productions of *Twelfth Night* Malvolio isn't visible at all behind this partition; in others he can be seen woefully trapped within his "madman's" cell.

Greeting Malvolio in the same portentous clergyman's tones, Feste immediately has the gullible steward believing that he is indeed "Sir Topas," the curate, and Malvolio who, by now, understands that something has gone wrong and that his amorous behavior hasn't brought the results he thought it would, begs for the priest's assistance. "Out, hyperbolical [extravagant] fiend!" is Feste's melodramatic reply. He ignores Malvolio as being a madman, incompetent to converse with anyone, and addresses, instead, the devil that presumably possesses him. When Malvolio bitterly complains that in being charged with lunacy he's been "wronged," the fool again unsympathetically responds with "Fie, thou dishonest Satan!"

Comment

Feste is at last having his long-awaited revenge on Malvolio for the cutting remarks that the arrogant steward made about his abilities as a wit in act 1, scene 5. We must remember that, though he was present when the plot against Malvolio was originally conceived, the fool has for some reason been absent during the ensuing sport with Olivia and her smiling yellow-stockinged, cross-gartered lover. Thus he's whole-heartedly enjoying this first chance he's had to personally reap the benefits of the plot and at every turn he "rubs it in" as much as possible that the unfortunate Malvolio can expect no help whatsoever in his plight from "Sir Topas," the priest.

When Malvolio complains that the room in which he's confined is dark "as Hell," the false "Sir Topas" responds that on the contrary it has windows "toward the south-north . . . as lustrous as ebony" - and that Malvolio must indeed be mad to say otherwise. Malvolio stubbornly insists that the room is dark (which it is) and Feste then solemnly tells him that the darkness in which he's "puzzled" is the darkness of ignorance. Malvolio begs the priest to "make the trial" of his sanity "in any constant question" (that is, let him prove he's sane by the clarity and force of his mind in logical argument.) This, of course, gives the fool just the opportunity he's looking for, and he quickly makes a hash of Malvolio (who indeed acquits himself quite sanely on the subject) with a lot of double-talk about Pythagoras, concluding with the advice that until Malvolio must be considered indubitably mad. believes in the Pythagorean doctrine of the transmigration of souls, he

Comment

Pythagoras was an early Greek philosopher who believed in reincarnation. He held that the human soul after death could pass into a beast or a bird as well as another human body. This, of course, was a belief commonly considered mad by the Elizabethans, and certainly (as now) regarded as entirely repulsive by the Church. Thus Feste, as "Sir Topas," is truly tormenting Malvolio by giving him a wholly unexpected answer when he supports Pythagoras's philosophy. Malvolio knows that the priest can't be really saying what he seems to be saying-yet he believes so firmly that Feste really is "Sir Topas" that the only answer left for him must be that he himself is indeed mad, and hearing things.

When "Sir Topas" has left the unfortunate steward-still unconsoled, in darkness-Sir Toby and Maria, who have witnessed the whole scene, congratulate him heartily on his performance. Then Sir Toby suggests that the fool visit Malvolio in his "own voice" (that is, address Malvolio in his natural voice) and find out without any further clowning how the steward really is. For, says Toby worriedly, he himself is now in so much trouble with his niece (on account of his run-in in the last scene with "Cesario") that he'd rather like to be finally rid of this plot altogether, before it backfires. On this note, he and Maria depart and Feste skips across the stage to Malvolio's prison once more, this time acting only as himself.

Singing a cheerful little song ("Hey robin, jolly robin,/ Tell me how thy lady does") the clown pretends to be just casually passing by, with no knowledge at all that Malvolio is confined nearby. When the miserable "madman" woefully calls to him for help - in tones significantly humbler and friendlier than the arrogant ones he'd used at their last encounter - Feste feigns surprise at hearing of his plight. Malvolio confides to him that he's been "notoriously abused" and isn't really mad at all, but just as sane as the fool himself. Feste, who can't resist teasing his old enemy a little longer, replies that "you are mad indeed if you be no better in your wits than a fool," and then goes on to introduce "Sir Topas" onto the scene once more. First he addresses Malvolio in his quavering, priestly voice, and then again in his light-hearted fool's tones. In an exhibition of his virtuosity as a performer, he carries on a little conversation with himself, greeting himself the priest ("God be wi' you, good Sir Topas") and then solemnly warning himself the fool not to carry on any conversation with a dangerous madman like Malvolio ("Maintain no words with him, good fellow").

Finally Feste drops this trickery, and pays a little more attention to Malvolio's pleas for assistance. His friend (and frequent benefactor) Sir Toby has, after all, indicated that he'd like to get the whole business over with, and Feste can help him by at least helping to release Malvolio from his prison. Hence he accedes to Malvolio's request to bring him "light and paper and ink" so that he can write a letter to Olivia-explaining just how he's been so abused. (The steward, of course, doesn't know the real authors of the plot against him, but he does think he'd better get the story of the letter straight with his mistress, especially since he still believes it came from her.) Feste promises, further, to convey the finished document to Olivia herself, and the two part with Malvolio extravagantly thanking him for his kindness and promising to "requite it in the highest degree." These words of humble gratitude can't help but be pleasant to the vengeful Feste, who skips merrily offstage, singing an appropriate little ditty about a "mad lad and the Devil."

SUMMARY

This scene is a purely comic one.

1. By returning us to the Malvolio plot, it provides some relief from the headlong romantic developments of the previous scene. It also provides a kind of breathing space during which the new relationship between Olivia and Sebastian can ripen further into love.

2. It satisfies our desire to see Malvolio get his comeuppance. Now that he's been so humbled-locked in a dark room and fed on bread and water-our sympathies begin to shift a little more toward him. He's no longer arrogant or unyielding in his behavior. Miserable and misunderstood, he's a pitiable figure, and we do, in fact, pity him. Thus the way is prepared for his eventual release and the final uncovering of the plot against him.

3. The way is also prepared for Malvolio's release by Sir Toby's fear of his niece's displeasure-which was aroused in act 3, scene 1 by his encounter with Sebastian. Now Toby is anxious to get rid of the whole Malvolio plot before his part in it is discovered and

he's really "turned out of doors" by Olivia as Maria and Malvolio have warned he will be someday.

4. Finally, this scene gives Feste a chance to exhibit his skill as a mimic, and to take his own private revenge on Malvolio for the steward's earlier scorn of him. He does this gleefully and then reluctantly expedites the **denouement** of this particular plot (as Toby had asked him to) by promising to bring Malvolio writing materials so that he can inform Olivia of his plight.

ACT 4: SCENE 3

This very brief scene (35 lines) takes place in Olivia's garden, where we discover Sebastian, alone and still puzzling over the strange situation in which he finds himself. He's evidently just come from his tete-a-tete with Olivia "within the house," where she'd taken him at the end of act 4, Scene 2, and he still finds his good fortune in so quickly winning the love of such a woman hard to believe. But, he concludes, on the evidence of his senses ("this is the air, that is the glorious sun") he's neither mad nor dreaming, so these events must be real. He wonders where Antonio can be, and thinks that his friend's advice might be helpful to him. We, of course, know that the loyal captain has been arrested.

Finally, he concludes that there must be some mistake in all this, or else he's mad, or the lady's mad. But he's already dismissed the idea that he himself might be mad - and as for Olivia being mad, she seems to be able to run her house smoothly enough, and command her servants with authority, things she couldn't do if she were really mad. So he's left again with the notion that something's wrong, but he doesn't know what. ("There's something in't/ That is deceivable. . .") Nevertheless, since he himself is by now in love with Olivia, he's quite willing to go along with whatever she may propose, no matter how obscure her reasons are. So when she herself enters with a priest, a moment later, and actually proposes marriage, he accedes gladly enough.

Comment

Olivia, who realizes that she's rushing things a bit ("Blame not this haste of mine..." she begins) herself finds recent developments hard to credit. "Cesario" - who she believes Sebastian to be-has always before rejected her romantic advances in no uncertain terms, so that when "his" coldness suddenly turns to warmth, she doesn't know what to think, and can hardly believe her good fortune. Underneath her confusion, however, her shrewd womanliness leads her to want to get her man while she can-since, if Cesario is capable of one such unexpected shift in feeling, he may well be capable of another.

She asks Sebastian to go at once with her and the priest to a nearby chapel, and recite the marriage vows so "that my most jealous and too doubtful soul May live at peace." The clergyman will, she promises, conceal the marriage until "Cesario" is willing to have it publicly announced.

To her surprise and delight, Sebastian readily agrees, promising that "having sworn truth" he "ever will be true." Overjoyed, Olivia calls on the Heavens to "shine" on her act, and the pair go off without further discussion to be wed.

SUMMARY

Though this is the shortest scene in the play, it's also one of the most important in bringing about the **denouement** of the romantic plot.

1. Olivia, mistaking Sebastian for Cesario - and still uncertain of his love, but delighted with the change in his attitude toward her-asks him to prove his good faith by marrying her. Their marriage, of course, provides the key to the events of act 5, in which the whole tangled skin of the romantic plot (based on the confusion of Viola's and Sebastian's identities) must be unravelled.

2. Sebastian has really fallen in love with the beautiful Olivia by now, and he recklessly agrees to marry her at once, even though he recognizes that there must be some mistake responsible for the suddenness with which she's made these romantic advances to him.

3. We learn from a casual remark of Sebastian's that he himself is perfectly loyal to Antonio (though Antonio, on the basis of Viola's behavior, will later accuse him of ingratitude). Sebastian has, in fact, actually kept their rendezvous at the Elephant, and was disturbed not to find Antonio there.

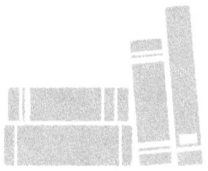

TWELFTH NIGHT

TEXTUAL ANALYSIS

ACT 5

....

ACT 5

This final scene of the play, a long and important one, takes place again in front of Olivia's house. Feste the fool and the servant Fabian enter first. Feste is carrying a letter (which, we can infer, is the one Malvolio has just written with his help to Olivia) and Fabian begs the clown to let him see it. Feste, who's promised Malvolio he'll personally deliver the letter to his lady, refuses. He himself is anxious by now to get the whole business over with, and he doesn't trust Fabian's intentions. Before Fabian can do more than mildly protest. Orsino, with his entire retinue-Viola, Curio, and a group of other attendants-appears on the scene.

Comment

Orsino and Olivia have been carefully kept apart for most of the play. In fact, their separation-as much as his own melodrama-has helped a good deal to give an air of unreality to the Duke's love-sickness. They're now being brought together onstage for the first time, for the **denouement** of the triangle in which they're involved.

Orsino addresses Feste and Fabian kindly, asking if they "belong" to the Lady Olivia. They reply in the affirmative and then, after a closer look at the fool, the Duke remembers that he himself is well-acquainted with Feste (who had, in fact, we may recall, been summoned to perform for him in act 2, scene 4). There follows some light banter between the two, in which Feste shows his wit to good advantage, cleverly proving, among other things, that he's "the better for my foes and the worst for my friends" - because his foes tell him the truth about himself whereas his friends "praise me and make an ass of me." When Orsino shows himself to be well-pleased with this "fooling," Feste redoubles his efforts and with an explosion of dazzling wit manages to beg two separate coins from the Duke. But Orsino refuses to give him a third until he fetches Olivia for him, so Feste hurries off at once to relay the news of this important visitor's arrival to his mistress.

At this moment, Antonio is brought in by the officers who arrested him at the end of act 3, scene 4. Both Viola and Orsino recognize him immediately, Viola as the man who rescued her from Andrew and Toby, and Orsino as the "salt-water thief" who inflicted so much damage on the noblest vessel of the Illyrian fleet in a recent sea-fight. The officers confirm that the captain is indeed "that Antonio/ That took the Phoenix and her fraught (cargo) from Candy (Crete)," and they tell Orsino that they caught the fellow brawling without any regard for law or his own safety "here on the streets." Curious, Orsino asks Antonio (calling him "notable pirate" and thief) what "foolish boldness" could have induced him to put himself within the reach of his bitter enemies in Illyria.

Antonio, denying that he's either a thief or a pirate, though (for reasons never given) Orsino's enemy, replies that "a witchcraft drew me hither," and goes on to tell the whole story of his relationship with Sebastian: how he'd rescued the boy from the "rude sea," followed him, purely out of love, into this hostile town, lent him his purse, rescued him from his adversaries (Andrew and Toby), and finally been treated by the youth (who refused to return his money) with the utmost ingratitude.

Viola exclaims that Antonio indeed "did her kindness" by drawing his sword in her defense, but as for the rest of his story, it must be madness. Orsino then asks Antonio when he and Sebastian had arrived in Illyria, hoping thus to shed some light on the mystery. When Antonio replies that they'd only arrived today, but had been together for three months before this, Orsino concludes that the man must indeed be mad, since the "youth" in question, Cesario-has attended him for the past three months.

At this point Olivia enters, and Orsino drops the problem of Antonio (telling the officers to "take him aside") to declare extravagantly that "Now Heaven walks on earth." Olivia-who is most anxious that the Duke not renew his suit-greets him coldly. Then, catching sight of Cesario (to whom she thinks she was married just a few hours ago), she exclaims "Cesario, you do not keep promise with me." Viola, mystified, starts to reply, but the Duke interrupts her. Olivia, more interested in Cesario's words, tries to silence "his" master, but Viola defers to her lord. ("My lord doth speak, my duty hushes me.") Olivia, annoyed, remarks contemptuously that if what Orsino has to say "be aught to the old tune" his words of love are really quite repulsive to her by now. "Still so cruel?" the Duke asks, rather angrily (he too is becoming annoyed) and "Still so constant" (in her rejection of him) is Olivia's reply. This prompts him to desperately ask her

("You uncivil lady,/ To whose . . . altars my soul the faithful'st offerings hath breath'd out") what he should do now. She answers indifferently that he should do what he pleases.

Olivia's coldness is by now too much for Orsino. In a rage of jealousy and frustration at her continued humiliating rejections of him, he swears that he'll revenge himself on her - either, like a famous Egyptian thief (Thyamis, who killed the girl that he'd kidnapped rather than let her fall into other hands) by killing what he loves or, better still, by taking Cesario away from her. Yes, he decides, perhaps it would be best to "sacrifice" Cesario, since he can see that it's really Cesario that Olivia loves. Much as he, too, loves Cesario, he declares, he'd willingly murder "him" to spite the "marble-breasted" Olivia.

Comment

As the absolute ruler of Illyria, Orsino has despotic powers of life and death over all his subjects. His announced willingness to exercise these powers for a personal whim-essentially out of spite-sheds further light on his melodramatic extravagance and romantic egotism.

Viola-whose own love for Orsino is apparently boundless - then declares that she'd willingly die "a thousand deaths" if that would make Orsino rest easier, and starts to follow him offstage. Olivia, in agitation, asks Cesario where "he's" going, and Viola replies that she's going "after him I love/ More than I love these eyes, more than my life,/ More, by all mores, than e'er I shall love wife" (a reasonable enough remark, since she could hardly love a "wife" anyway). Olivia, who imagines that she herself is already "Cesario's" wife, exclaims that she's been "beguiled" (deceived) by the "youth", otherwise he wouldn't forget his recent vows so easily. When Viola asks her what she's talking about, she calls him "husband," and at this the Duke, furious, intervenes to ask Cesario what the truth of the matter is. Viola repeats that she doesn't know what Olivia's talking about.

Comment

The last ten lines of this bitter exchange are rhymed, and the rhyming-as well as the shortness of the speeches-contributes considerably to the mounting tension of the scene. e.g.:

Duke: Come, away!

Olivia: Whither, my lord? Cesario, husband, stay.

Duke: Husband!

Olivia: Aye, husband. Can he that deny?

Duke: Her husband, sirrah!

Viola: No, my lord, not I.

This, after all, is the **climax** of the complicated romantic plot of *Twelfth Night* and Shakespeare uses every means he can-in the style as well as the content of the language-to emphasize the drama of the confrontation.

Olivia, rationalizing that Cesario's fear of the Duke's power and importance is making "him" deny "his" recent marriage in such a cowardly way, urges "him" to admit the truth, since "he," as her "husband," will be just as important as Orsino. There's no need for this timidity, she declares, and then calls on the priest (who's been summoned by a servant) to verify that he did, in fact, just marry her to "Cesario." When the priest confirms that such a marriage took place not two hours before this scene, Orsino, enraged, begins to upbraid Cesario for "his" falseness, and finally dismisses "him" forever from his service: "Farewell, and take her," he cries furiously, "but direct thy feet/Where thou and I henceforth may never meet."

Viola starts to protest, but Olivia, still sure that Cesario is motivated only by fear of the Duke's wrath, tries to stop "him." At just this moment of excruciating tension, Sir Andrew Aguecheek, bloody, battered, and calling loudly for a surgeon, hobbles in.

Comment

Andrew and Toby are obviously introduced at this point not only as a plot mechanism to help get Sebastian onstage, but also to provide some comic relief from the almost unbearable tension which has been building up without remission since the beginning of the scene between the three romantic principals.

Distracted from her own troubles for a moment by Sir Andrew's obvious misery, Olivia turns to question him, and he declares that his head has been broken - and Sir Toby's too! - by the "Count's gentleman," Cesario. "We took him for a coward," Andrew complains, "but he's the very Devil incarnate." Orsino, astounded, looks inquiringly at the innocent Viola, who denies all knowledge of the affair. When Andrew sees this gentle Cesario, he immediately confuses him with the other, ferocious "Cesario" (in reality, of course, Sebastian) who's just beaten him up, and begins to bitterly repeat his accusations. Again Viola denies them, remarking that Andrew drew his sword on her "without cause," but that she had treated him politely and not hurt him (in Act 3, Scene 4). "If a bloody coxcomb (head) be a hurt, you have hurt me," declares the injured knight indignantly.

At this moment in staggers Toby, supported by the fool, and obviously as much damaged as his friend. Toby's obviously drunk, as usual (and, indeed, Andrew maintains that if he hadn't been drunk he would certainly have done more harm to Cesario), and he seems to be bearing his hurt philosophically. He asks for a surgeon to dress his wounds, and the clown merrily tells him that the surgeon has been drunk for an hour and isn't available. "I hate a drunken rogue," comments the drunken Toby.

Olivia-who seems to be fond of her renegade relative despite his awful behavior-orders Feste to help the two knights to bed and get them medical attention, and the three groaningly depart, with Fabian assisting too. As they leave, Toby expresses his pain by heaping extravagant insults on the unlucky Andrew (who is, he says, "an asshead and a coxcomb and a knave, a thin-faced knave, a gull!")

As soon as they're gone, Sebastian himself, the other, ferocious "Cesario," puts in an appearance, apologizing profusely to Olivia for having hurt her kinsman. He sees that she's looking strangely at him (because there are now two Cesarios on stage.) and assuming it's because she's offended by his wounding of Toby, he explains that he couldn't help himself because the two knights struck first. Still, he says he's sorry, especially in the light of the marriage vows he and the Countess so recently exchanged. Dumb-founded, Olivia, Orsino, Antonio, and the others onstage look from Viola to Sebastian, not knowing what to make of this sudden incredible duplication of "Cesario!"

Comment

This is the **climax** of *Twelfth Night*, the moment toward which the complicated mistaken-identity plot has been building. In fact, as we've seen, the whole romantic plot itself - and much of the comic plot-is based on the intricate series of errors and misunderstandings which Viola's male disguise, and her twin brother's unexpected appearance in Illyria, make possible.

Sebastian now catches sight of Antonio, and with extravagant expressions of love and loyalty, he tells his friend how worried he's been about him since he failed to keep their rendezvous at the Elephant. Antonio, almost speechless with wonder, asks Sebastian how he has "made division of" himself. Pointing to Viola, he remarks that "an apple cleft in two, is not more twin/ Than these two creatures." Sebastian now notices Viola for the first time, and he is himself amazed by the sight, since he doesn't of course, know that his sister is alive and, furthermore, dressed as a man. "Do I stand there?" he asks, astonished, and then goes on to declare that he never had a (twin) brother, though he did have a sister, recently lost at sea. Who are you? he asks Viola. "What name? What parentage?"

Viola, near tears with joy, explains that Sebastian of Messaline was her father, and that she had a brother named Sebastian who went, looking just like this present Sebastian, to his "watery tomb." Sebastian, now beginning to see the light, tells Viola that if she only were a woman, he "should my tears let fall upon your cheek,/ And say 'thrice welcome, drowned Viola!'" And after exchanging a few more pertinent facts about themselves, the two do fall weeping into each other's arms, as soon as Viola declares that she is, in fact, a woman, and can take

Sebastian to "a captain in this town" who has been keeping her female garments for her while she masquerades as Cesario.

> Comment

This meeting between Sebastian and Viola is really a very moving scene. Viola, of course, knows that Sebastian is really her brother, so our attention is concentrated on Sebastian, as he wrestles with the problem of his double's identity. He has no brother and at first doesn't even suspect that Cesario might be his sister, but gradually he comes to understand that "he" must indeed be Viola. Viola's tender acceptance of Sebastian's confusion, and Sebastian's delight in finding her alive, make their final recognition of each other truly dramatic and poignant. (Such a scene, incidentally, obviously essential to the **denouement** of the mistaken identity plots of which the Elizabethans were so fond, is officially called a recognition scene.)

Finally, convinced at last that his sister is alive, in the guise of Cesario, Sebastian turns, rather amused, to Olivia, and points out to her that she's actually married the wrong person, but that anyway, in this case the wrong person was really the right person, since the Countess would otherwise "have been contracted to a maid!"

Orsino now decides that he too must "share in this most happy wreck," and turning to Viola (the two couples are finally pairing off in the proper way) he asks her if she meant it when she swore so often that she never would love a woman as she loved him. (He too, is beginning to see the light about Viola, now that her true identity is known.) Viola happily assures him that she did mean it, and will gladly take the same oath again a hundred times over. Touched, and realizing, perhaps, that his

Platonic love for the beautiful boy, Cesario, could just as easily become a romantic passion for the lovely, good-humored girl, Viola, Orsino takes her hand and asks to see her in her woman's clothes. Viola explains that the captain who's been keeping them for her has been thrown in jail on some suit of Malvolio's, and so Olivia immediately calls for her steward to explain the matter further and get the captain released as soon as possible.

But now, of course, she suddenly remembers about Malvolio's madness, a problem which she'd completely forgotten for the time being in her absorption with her own romantic madness. At this point, Feste and Fabian conveniently appear, with the steward's letter, which the clown immediately delivers to his mistress, explaining that he wasn't supposed to give it to her yet, but he doesn't really think it matters very much just when "a madman's epistles" are delivered. Olivia orders him to open it and read it to her" - but when he can't **refrain** from reciting its contents in a melodramatically "mad" tone, she turns to Fabian and asks him to read it. This servant agreeably does his mistress' bidding and in a straightforward manner reads Malvolio's note which proves surprisingly sane. In it, he angrily informs Olivia that he is not mad, and that he resents having been put thus into the power of her "drunken cousin" Toby, especially since it was her own letter which induced him to behave as he did. Both Olivia and Orsino agree that Malvolio's words don't sound mad, and Olivia orders Fabian to "bring him hither."

While Fabian is gone on his errand, she turns (for the first time) in a friendly way to Orsino, and asks how he'd feel about having her for a sister-which he would if he'd marry Viola as she has married Sebastian. Orsino, nothing loath, at once proposes to the former Cesario, declaring that for all the service she's done him, "so far beneath (her) soft and tender breeding," he will now make her "master's mistress." Viola is, of course, overjoyed, and

Olivia, glad enough now to simply be friends with this original Cesario since she's acquired "his" double, Sebastian, for her very own, exclaims enthusiastically "A sister! You are she."

At this point-now that everything's been settled in the romantic plot-Fabian returns with the long-suffering Malvolio, who immediately begins to protest the injuries he's received at Olivia's hands. When the Countess maintains that she's never done him any wrong, he produces the famous letter, insisting that she can't deny it's in her own handwriting. He then goes on to ask her why she gave him such "clear lights of favor" - bidding him come smiling, cross-gartered and yellow-stockinged to her, etc. - and then allowed him to be imprisoned in a dark room, treated as a madman by the priest, and "made the most notorious geck (fool) and gull" ever.

Olivia, who's been perusing the letter in question throughout Malvolio's recital of his grievances, replies that unfortunately the handwriting is not hers, but Maria's, and promises a full inquiry into the whole business, at which the wronged steward can be "both the plaintiff and the judge."

Comment

Despite Malvolio's many unpleasant personality traits, Olivia values him highly as a servant. As we've seen, he's remarkably efficient, and his coolness and arrogance have often stood her in good stead when she needed to get rid of an unwanted visitor or handle a difficult matter with dispatch. Thus she's willing to go to almost any lengths-even, perhaps, to sacrifice Maria-in order to placate him.

At this point, however, Fabian loyally comes to the little servingwoman's defense. He confesses that he and Toby are solely responsible for the plot against Malvolio (which, of course, isn't really true) and that they were motivated by some just grievances they had against the arrogant steward (which is true). He declares, further, that Maria had written the letter only at Sir Toby's insistence, and then informs the assembled company that as a reward the jovial knight has finally married her.

Comment

The (offstage) union of Maria and Toby balances out the pairing-off process with which the action concludes. Not only on a romantic level are all the problems of the play resolved by marriage, but also on a comic level. In one sense, of course, the match between Toby and Maria is the most unheralded in the work, since whatever feelings there may be between the fun-loving pair they are nowhere near as important as, say, those between Orsino and Viola-but in another sense, their marriage is the most inevitable, since no other romantic complications could possibly have prevented it.

Olivia hears Fabian's speech sympathetically enough, and then, more amused than not, turns to the hapless Malvolio exclaiming with pity "Poor fool, how they have baffled (disgraced) thee!" This arouses Feste-who still holds a grudge against the steward-to mockingly quote a few lines from Maria's letter and then, worse still, to use his "Sir Topas" voice, revealing the true identity of the "priest" who had so tortured Malvolio in his dark jail. "And thus the whirligig of time brings in his revenges," Feste can't help jeering. "I'll be revenged on the whole pack of you," Malvolio shouts in reply, and rushes furiously offstage.

Orsino-as befits the ruler of this confused kingdom-orders some servants to pursue Malvolio, and try to placate him, especially since the angry steward hasn't yet given them the information they want about Viola's friend, the captain. In the meantime, Orsino declares, he and his party will remain at Olivia's house to celebrate the happy outcome of recent events, and as soon as Viola can be dressed in more feminine clothes, he'll crown her "Orsino's mistress and his fancy's Queen."

On this note, the entire company departs, except for Feste, who remains behind to sing a short sad song, which begins "When that I was and a little boy,/ With hey ho, the wind and the rain,/ A foolish thing was but a toy,/ For the rain it raineth every day." The little ballad goes on to outline the progress of the singer's life - from youth, to manhood, to death (always repeating the mournful **refrain** about the wind and the rain, ballad-fashion, at the middle and end of every **stanza**), and it finally concludes by informing the audience with sad courtesy that "A great while ago, the world begun,/ With hey ho, the wind and the rain,/ But that's all one, our play is done,/ And we'll strive to please you every day."

Comment

Shakespeare often liked to end his romantic comedies, not on a note of unmitigated triumph and celebration, but on a note of sadness and questioning, with a mournful little **ballad** like the one Feste sings here. After all the romantic complications and all the comic convolutions, these final poignant lyrics seem to suggest, what is there really left that matters? Now that the fuss is over, what did it all amount to, anyway? Nothing more than "midsummer madness," a brief dream of love and merrymaking. Nothing more than a little exercise in "foolery" in honor of the *Twelfth Night* holiday. Nothing more than What You, the audience, Will it to be.

SUMMARY

In this long, final scene of the play, which takes up an entire act, all the loose ends of the action are neatly tied together.

1. Orsino is finally brought to Olivia's house, where the melancholy Countess once more rejects her melancholy suitor in no uncertain terms.

2. Viola, whose difficult situation in Illyria has been further complicated by the presence of her twin-brother, Sebastian, becomes the target of everyone's wrath. Accusations are flung at her from all sides.

    (a) Olivia, who has just married Sebastian, calls her "husband," thinking she's "Cesario," and begs "him" to acknowledge her as "his" wife.

    (b) Orsino, enraged at his servant's perfidy, threatens to banish "him."

    (c) Antonio, who is brought in by the officers who arrested him earlier, again accuses Viola of ingratitude for not returning his purse (thinking she's Sebastian).

    (d) Sir Andrew Aguecheek, who, along with Olivia's cousin Toby, has been hurt in a duel with the real Sebastian, accuses Viola of having wounded him, and threatened to bring a law suit against her.

3. Viola once more shows

    (a) her love for Orsino, and her loyalty to him, by proclaiming her willingness to die "a thousand deaths" if it will set his mind at rest.

    (b) She also shows her intelligence (she's figured out that her brother must really be alive, and the cause of all her troubles) and her solicitude for Sebastian, by keeping quiet about her true identity until he's had a chance to work things out himself.

4. The romantic triangle is resolved by Orsino's decision to marry Viola, now that he knows she's really a girl. Events were leading up to this all along-Orsino's ready affection for Cesario makes it quite believable that he should love Viola enough to make her his wife, and Viola's long-suffering love for the Duke makes her joyful acceptance of his proposal just as inevitable. Thus three of the melancholy lovers-Viola, Orsino and Olivia-are relieved of their melancholy by the appearance of Sebastian. Both Olivia and Viola get the men they'd wanted all along; Sebastian gets his sister back, and a beautiful wife into the bargain; and Orsino gets a lovely mistress, which is all he ever wanted anyway, since he was always more in love with love that specifically with Olivia herself.

5. Now that the romantic plot has been untangled, Shakespeare can turn his attention to unravelling the comic plot:

(a) Malvolio is released from prison, since the scheme against him has gone about as far as it can go. The plotters-Fabian, Toby, Andrew, and Maria, as well as Feste,-have all had their revenge, and the arrogant steward is once more let loose in the world, this time to plan his revenge against them. He has, however, learned a good lesson about the pitfalls into which unbridled ambition and egotism can lead.

(b) Sir Toby and Sir Andrew also get their comeuppance, in this case for having unjustifiably challenged the innocent Viola. Sebastian-a far fiercer "Cesario" than his sister could ever be-wounds both Olivia's unscrupulous cousin, and his feebly egotistical friend, in a return match.

(c) Maria is rewarded for her schemes and efforts at merrymaking by a marriage to Sir Toby, a match for which she's evidently been striving for quite a while.

(d) Finally, Feste's sad little song, addressed to the audience, leaves us with a feeling that all these tangles and triangles have been no more than fun and games, entertaining and delightful, but merely "matter for a May morning."

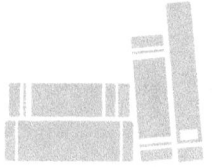

TWELFTH NIGHT

CHARACTER ANALYSES

VIOLA

Viola is one of Shakespeare's most charming and admirable heroines, and certainly the most sympathetic of the major "serious" characters (Orsino, Olivia, and herself) in *Twelfth Night*. Though she's forced to disguise herself as a page, for safety's sake, she's apparently as well-born as Olivia is - the daughter of Sebastian of Messaline, a highly-placed nobleman in his own land. She's also very attractive physically - which can be inferred from the fact that even in male attire she's graceful enough for Orsino to comment on her good looks.

But perhaps the most attractive aspect of Viola - to a modern audience, at least - is her vigorous, good-humored, unpretentious personality. Unlike Olivia, whose counterpart and opposite she is, she makes no melodramatic plans to mourn her brother's apparent death with extravagant gestures. Instead, her grief is quiet, deep, sincere - and tinged with hope that Sebastian may still be alive. Furthermore, finding herself in a difficult, perhaps compromising position in a strange country, she spends little time bemoaning the harshness of her fate, but immediately sets to work with characteristic practical energy to figure out a way to improve her situation. When she enters Orsino's service, her talent, wit, and good looks quickly captivate him, just as, soon after, when she's sent to "woo" Olivia, these qualities also entrance the Countess. Indeed, in almost every scene in which she appears - whether she's jesting with Feste, quietly philosophizing with Orsino, or gracefully flattering Olivia-Viola's courtly skill and down-to-earth charm are clearly evident. Most of all, when she herself falls deeply, and apparently hopelessly, in love with Orsino, though she feels very strongly the frustration and pain of her position (disguised as a boy, but perfectly able to love like a woman) her justifiable melancholy is neither extravagant, like Olivia's, nor egotistical, like Orsino's. She does her best at all times to conceal it, and we can't help respecting her for her determination to sit "like Patience on a monument," always putting the best face on things and always, whenever possible, "smiling at grief."

Olivia

Though basically a noble, generous, passionate woman, Olivia has many more faults than Viola has. Indeed, Shakespeare probably meant us to regard the two as emotional opposites, or at least as counterparts of each other, Thus Olivia's name may be considered an anagram (rearrangement) of Viola's, since it contains all the same letters (with an extra i), and Olivia's problems (the loss of a brother, an unwanted courtship, and unrequited love) are also the same as Viola's. But the Illyrian lady's reaction to these difficulties is very different from the energetic young "page's." Olivia seems to have been much more spoiled than Viola, and as Viola herself points out, she is too proud," as well as too extravagant by nature. She melodramatically resolves to mourn her brother's death for seven years - and in that space of time, never to leave the house.

Viola, on the other hand, reacts more calmly and sensibly, though no less sorrowfully, to the possibility that Sebastian may have been killed. She coldly, and rather unsympathetically rejects Orsino's proposals of marriage, but Viola is a little more compassionate in her reaction to Olivia's own avowals of love. Finally, she falls passionately and wholeheartedly in love with "Cesario," and is unable to restrain herself from impulsively declaring her feelings for the "youth" almost at the first opportunity. (Viola, in contrast, comes close to confessing her love for Orsino, but her iron self-control doesn't weaken in the end.)

Despite all her faults, however, Olivia has many redeeming good qualities. She's undeniably beautiful and intelligent. More important, she's generous and wise in the rule of her household, as her basically kind treatment of both the drunken Toby and the "mad" Malvolio attests. Furthermore, though she herself is essentially serious - and throughout *Twelfth Night*, melancholy - she has a sense of humor and can appreciate true wit wherever she finds it, whether in the page "Cesario," or in Feste, the jester. In sum, she's a real aristocrat: courtly and noble in her bearing; a little self-absorbed, spoiled and proud, because of the importance of her position; but beneath a haughty exterior "generous, guiltless and of free disposition."

Maria

Olivia's clever, witty servingwoman - really a kind of lady-in-waiting - is supposed to be exceptionally small, and as quick and sharp in her movements as in her ideas. We're informed about her height and her delicacy by a number of references. For instance, Sir Toby describes her as "the youngest wren of nine," and as a "little villain." In another place, he ironically calls her "Penthesilea" (the Queen of the Amazons, and Viola, with the same ironic intention, calls her "giant."

But besides being small and shrewd, Maria is fun-loving and frolicsome, almost as ready as Sir Toby (on whom she has marital designs) to make merry, though with much more of a regard for the proprieties. Indeed, throughout the play she's torn between her loyalty to Olivia and her sense of the dignity of the household (the disapproving "By my troth, Sir Toby, you must come in earlier o' nights!" is her first line in the play) and her fondness for Toby and desire to please him. The latter desire-probably fortified by a keen interest in the jolly knight's money and social position-wins out, and Maria invents the anti-Malvolio plot, the chief comic action of the play, at least in part to make Toby happy. Of course, the wonderful sport of "gulling" Malvolio (for whom she's conceived an implacable dislike) makes Maria herself happy too, and in the end, having made her choice between Olivia and Toby, she gets her reward-Olivia's very mild displeasure, and Toby's hand in marriage.

Orsino

Orsino is the only "serious" male character whom we get to know at all well. The others - Sebastian, Antonio, the Sea Captain, etc. - are all rather shadowy. But Orsino is a very real and realistic person, anything but the handsome, idealized monarch of a fairytale kingdom. He is handsome, of course, and as Olivia says "I suppose him virtuous, know him noble,/ Of great estate, of fresh and stainless youth;/ In voices - [languages] well divulged [well-educated], free, learned, and valiant; And in dimension and the shape of nature,/ A gracious person." It is, in fact, these qualities which make it possible for Viola to fall in love with the Duke so quickly and so irrevocably.

Yet even so, they aren't the most important part of his personality, for Orsino, more than being a brave man or a handsome or a learned man, is a young, egotistical and rather affected man. In this sense, he's much like Olivia: just as she nurses her "grief" for her brother, he nurses his infatuation for her. This love of his, of course, is no more true love, like Viola's than Romeo's "love" for Rosalind was true love. Romeo had to meet Juliet to feel the real thing, and so Orsino is fated not to know the meaning of love until he really meets his page, "Cesario," as Viola, her real self. In the meantime, however, like all idle, extravagant, passionate young men, he spends much time sighing windily for an unattainable "beloved," and again, like Olivia, he's consumed with the sort of melancholy that was fashionable among aristocrats in Shakespeare's day.

Indeed, perhaps even more than Olivia, Orsino is a **parody** of an aristocrat, with his languid craving for music, his fanciful philosophizing on the nature of love, and even his spiteful, despotic willingness to "sacrifice the lamb that I do love ("Cesario") to revenge himself on Olivia for rejecting him. All this, like Olivia's behavior, is meant to contrast with Viola's true nobility, level-headedness and self-restraint. But at least in the end Orsino, again like Olivia, recovers a kind of balance, and in his dealings with Malvolio and his quick acceptance of Viola as a bride (he'd loved her all along, anyway, in her guise of a page) he shows a basic strain of goodwill and good sense.

Sebastian

Sebastian is essentially a male version of Viola, with all the differences in their personalities stemming from the difference in their sex. For one thing, of course, he's her twin, and so he's every bit as physically attractive as she is-which can be seen not only from the fact that Olivia loves him as passionately as she does "Cesario" (thinking, in fact, that he is "Cesario") but also from the comments Antonio makes about his good looks. Second, and perhaps even more important, he's just as charming, with as much personal magnetism, as Viola, which can also be seen from his relationship with Antonio. Further, he's as loyal as she is (both to Antonio and to Olivia, as well as, naturally, to Viola herself), and as practical, energetic and high-spirited, which can be seen from his enthusiastic desire to "do" the town as soon as he arrives in Illyria. As for the differences between sister and brother: Sebastian is, of course, much fiercer and more aggressive-e.g. in his duel with Andrew and Toby. And, naturally, he's able to respond with wholly masculine delight (as Viola certainly could not) to the beautiful Olivia's romantic advances. In short, though Sebastian is really a minor character, we learn a good deal about him in the course of the play, partly through his own actions and partly from the way in which his personality reflects Viola's.

Antonio

Loyal, generous, impulsive and courageous are the four adjectives which best describe Sebastian's rescuer, the good-hearted, brawling sea-captain Antonio. He's loyal throughout to his young friend, Sebastian, and generous, too, in his treatment of the boy-lending him his purse when he thinks he may be in need, besides apparently having maintained the youth at his own expense for several months after rescuing him from drowning. His impulsiveness shows both in the quick and deep affection he conceives for the boy, and in his loyally following Sebastian to Illyria, even against the young man's wishes. His courage, of course, is clear from the fact that he'd brave such hostile territory to join his friend, as well as from his ready intercession in the duel between Viola and Andrew. Finally, his courage may be inferred from his outstanding feats in the sea-fight against Illyria, even though Orsino accuses him (whether rightly or wrongly we don't know) of having been a "pirate" and a "saltwater thief," on that occasion. In any case, we can be sure that because of his kindness to Sebastian - and, even more, because of his (unwitting) generosity to Orsino's future "Queen," he'll be quickly enough forgiven for whatever his past transgressions may have been.

Feste

Feste has been called Shakespeare's "most musical" fool. Less witty than Touchstone in *As You Like It* and less profound, perhaps, than the fool in *King Lear*, he's nevertheless a highly accomplished jester-clever, polished and perceptive enough for Viola to remark of him that "This fellow is wise enough to play the fool,/ And to do that well, craves a kind of wit./ He must observe their moods on whom he jests,/ The quality of persons, and the time." Shakespeare is thought to have written the part for Robert Armin, a famous comedian of the day who'd recently joined the playwright's acting troupe. Armin was more musical and, in certain respects, more serious than the jester he succeeded, and hence the musical quality of Feste's part.

Still, Feste's comic accomplishments are numerous too. His fussy parodies of learning make even the melancholy Olivia laugh, and his talent for mimicry (in the "Sir Topas" scene) convulses Maria and Toby, and completely deceives Malvolio. But besides being musical, shrewd and funny, Feste is shown to have a real personality of his own. His hatred for Malvolio, conceived when the steward insults him in act 1, scene 5, motivates much of the comic subplot, and even by the end of the play he hasn't quite rid himself of the desire for revenge-as his last taunting words to Malvolio reveal. Indeed, throughout the play, like any good fool, Feste is all things to all men, besides seeming to be, literally, everywhere-singing songs for the Duke, cheering up Olivia when she's sad, plotting with Toby and his friends, squabbling with Malvolio, and even disinterestedly commenting to the audience, in his final song, on the silliness of it all. Because of this, he acts as a perfect link between the serious characters, Orsino, Olivia and Viola, for whom he performs, and the comic characters, Toby, Andrew and Maria, with whom he carouses.

Sir Toby Belch

Sir Toby Belch, Olivia's riotous relative (really her uncle, though he's often called "cousin" in the general fashion of the day) is the chief comic character and certainly the chief comic conspirator in *Twelfth Night*. The Elizabethan *Twelfth Night* celebration, which corresponded to the feast of the Epiphany, coming twelve days after Christmas, was often organized and dominated by a jolly person called the Lord of Misrule, who was in charge of the frolics and pranks that were so popular at this time of year. Many modern critics have quite naturally seen in Sir Toby Shakespeare's embodiment, in a play written expressly for the *Twelfth Night* festivities, of this same Lord of Misrule. Certainly Toby fits all the requirements of the part exactly. Hard-drinking, healthy, strong-willed, jovial and fond of every kind of merrymaking-plots, puns and brawls as well as wine, women and song-he's equaled among Shakespeare's own creations only by Sir John Falstaff, that similarly jolly loose-liver who was so popular in the *Henry IV* plays that Shakespeare wrote another whole play (*The Merry Wives of Windsor*) just for him. Perhaps, indeed, the playwright was trying once again to recapture his success with Falstaff in "*Twelfth Night*'s Lord of Misrule. In any case, Toby's antics are always a hit with audiences, though an Elizabethan audience probably appreciated them even more than we do today.

Of course, Toby has many faults, too. For one thing, his treatment of poor Sir Andrew Aguecheek is notably unscrupulous: he keeps the foolish knight around primarily to have the use of his money, and secondarily to tease and "gull" him (as in the first scene with Maria, or, more, in the duel episode.) Further, he is undoubtedly a "sot" (drunkard) and a noisy, rather boorish individual. He does, as Malvolio accuses him of doing, "make an alehouse" of Olivia's house, keeping late hours and violating the peace of the establishment with his "tinker's catches" and drinking songs bawled at the top of his lungs at three in the morning. His feelings for Maria, too, are not very romantic: he's more pleased by her cleverness as a comic co-worker than by any feminine attractions she may have. Still, he's a cheerful enough - and certainly an amusing enough-old souse, quite suited, with his high spirits and his conspiratorial energy, to act as *Twelfth Night*'s Lord of Misrule. And as Mark Van Doren has pointed out, "old households harbor such old men. They are nuisances to be endured because they are symbols of enduringness, signs of the family's great age." The aristocratic Olivia would no more turn her boisterous uncle out, as Malvolio threatens she would, than she'd lose the efficient steward himself.

Sir Andrew Aguecheek

Sir Andrew is perhaps the easiest character in *Twelfth Night* to understand, and the one, indeed, who is most a caricature and least an individualized character. Quite simply, he is a fool-not a "fool" in the sense of jester, like Feste, but a fool in the modern sense of an idiot. He's attached himself to Sir Toby for various reasons—mainly because he believes in Toby's unscrupulous encouragement of his hopeless courtship of Olivia. But further, he quite reasonably admires Toby's high spirits and noisy courage—qualities which he himself emphatically lacks. For besides being stupid, Sir Andrew is a coward: in the duel scene he behaves with every bit as much cowardice as the naturally shrinking, feminine Viola, despite all his boasted training as a knight. Only when he realizes that "Cesario" is a coward too, does he begin to lose some of his fear. Finally, Andrew is an egotist—as much of an egotist, as much deluded by vanity and self-love, as those other notable egotists, Malvolio and Orsino. It is his egotism which lets Toby convince him that Olivia will have him; his vanity which is piqued with jealousy at Viola's courtly skill; and his shallow self-love which enables him to write his silly, puffed-up challenge to "Cesario." In short, as Toby at last brutally tells him, he is "an ass-head, and a coxcomb, and a knave; a thin-faced knave, a gull."

Malvolio

As Maria notes fairly early in the play, Malvolio, Olivia's coldly efficient steward, is a "kind of Puritan." Indeed, like the other comic characters, he seems to be rather more closely based on certain Elizabethan social types than any of the serious characters are. Some modern scholars have even conjectured that he was meant as a **parody** of Queen Elizabeth's chief Comptroller (steward), Sir William Knollys. At any rate, whatever the case may be, Malvolio's personality is of such dominating importance to *Twelfth Night* that King James I is said to have renamed the play Malvolio.

Certainly Malvolio has many of the characteristics of the Puritans, those representatives of the rising middle-class who were so hateful to aristocratic merrymakers like Sir Toby and Sir Andrew, so looked-down-upon by true aristocrats like Olivia, and so disliked by carefree artists like Feste, or even Shakespeare himself. But despite his priggishness and his self-righteous complaints about Sir Toby's boisterous behavior, Malvolio is not purely a Puritan at all. As Maria, again, notes, he's basically an "affection'd [affected] ass" - and Olivia, too, sees that he is "sick of [with] self-love." This egotistical self-love, as well as his vain ambition, makes him very willing to cast off his severe, Puritanical ways at the slightest hint that more raucous behavior might give him a good chance to become Olivia's lover. Even before he receives the "anonymous" letter Maria plants, Malvolio is deep in luxuriously un-Puritanical daydreams of being married to his mistress; after he finds the letter, of course, he goes off the deep end entirely, crazily cross-gartering his legs, smiling and kissing his hand at the astonished Olivia, in the "mad" belief that he might be a suitable suitor for her. Indeed, in this sense Malvolio's "madness" is no joke-for such extravagant egotism, even more than his earlier, Puritanical pomposity, is truly a form of madness.

Fabian

We learn little about Fabian in *Twelfth Night*, beyond the fact that he's a quick-witted, good-natured servant, as fond as Toby and Maria of a good joke but rather more restrained in his pursuit of such pleasures. He's introduced into the action rather late, and for the most part he comments on the plots which others have set in motion, rather than directly participating. He does try to quiet Toby's and Andrew's out-of-bounds behavior in the garden scene, however, and he obviously enjoys tormenting poor "Cesario" in the duel scene. In the end, he bravely and responsibly takes much of the blame for the Malvolio plot onto himself-yet we can be sure that Olivia, knowing Toby's tendencies as a plotter, will not blame the basically innocent Fabian too harshly at all.

Minor Characters

All we know of the Sea Captain who rescued Viola is that he was kind and friendly, introducing the girl as a page to Orsino, and keeping both her secret and her clothes for the length of her stay at court as "Cesario." As for Orsino's gentlemen, Curio and Valentine, they are the usual courtly servants, elegant, polite and ever anxious for their ruler's best advantage in the world, as well as for the slightest marks of personal favor from him to themselves.

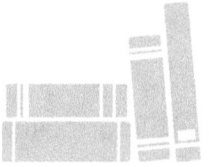

TWELFTH NIGHT

CRITICAL COMMENTARY

EARLY

The earliest "critical" comment on *Twelfth Night* is by one John Manningham, a play goes of the day, who wrote as follows in his diary of 1602: "At our feast we had a play called 'Twelve Night, or What You Will', much like the Commedy of Errores, or Menechmi in Plautus, but most like and neere to that in Italian called Inganni. A good practice in it to make the Steward believe his Lady widow was in love with him, by counterfeiting a letter as from his Lady in general terms, telling him what she liked best in him, and prescribing his gesture in smiling, his apparel, &c., and then when he came to practice making him believe they took him to be mad." This emphasis of Manningham's on the character of Malvolio foreshadowed the thought of many critics, including that of King James I, who actually had the play retitled Malvolio.

Just half a century later, however, another, much more famous diarist, the renowned Samuel Pepys, commented on three separate occasions that he thought *Twelfth Night* "one of the weakest plays that ever I saw on the stage." And Dr. Johnson, a century or so after him, wasn't exactly transported by the work either, remarking with typical eighteenth-century dogmatism that "The marriage of Olivia, and the succeeding perplexity, though well enough contrived to divert in the stage, wants credibility, and fails to produce the proper instruction required in the drama, as it exhibits no just picture of life." Of course, it wasn't ever Shakespeare's aim to produce a "just picture of life" in Dr. Johnson's sense, but the good doctor-usually a very receptive critic of the Elizabethan's works-simply couldn't, in this case, stomach the "madness" and fantasy of Illyria.

ROMANTICISM

To the romantic Charles Lamb, on the other hand, *Twelfth Night* was a thrilling piece of theater - and it's interesting to note that he restored Malvolio to the pre-eminent position in which such earlier critics as Manningham and King James I had placed him. Indeed, Lamb hardly thought Malvolio a comic character at all. "Malvolio," he wrote, "is not essentially ludicrous. He becomes comic but by accident. He is cold, austere, repelling; but dignified, consistent, and, for what appears, rather of an overstretched morality . . . But his morality and his manners are misplaced in Illyria. He is opposed to the proper levities of the piece, and falls in the unequal contest. Still his pride, or his gravity . . . is inherent, and native to the man, not mock or affected . . . His quality is the best unlovely, but neither buffoon nor contemptible. His bearing is lofty, a little above his station, but probably not much above his deserts. We see no reason why he should not have been brave, honorable, accomplished . . ."

This was a typically romantic view of Olivia's steward, and one shared, to a certain extent, by the American critic William Winter, who wrote, toward the end of the nineteenth century, that "People laugh at Malvolio, but they miss the meaning of him if they are not made to think as well as to laugh. For Malvolio is a person of serious individuality; a capable person, and one of ruminant mind and austere temperament. The mirth that is derived from him is derived by devices of mischief,-as when a sportive boy decorates a marble statue with a stovepipe hat. No plight can be more laughable than that of the pompous ass whose pomposity is made the direct means of his ridiculous disgrace. Malvolio falls into that plight and becomes ludicrously absurd, but his discomfiture is due to one of the chronic frailties of human nature, a frailty which, in him and by means of him, it is the purpose of the poet kindly and humorously to expose and rebuke."

By Malvolio's "frailty" Winter meant his grotesque egotism, and his ideas about the steward were thus a little more balanced and a good deal more accurate than Lamb's. For despite the earnest argument of the Englishman, Malvolio is hardly a tragic figure. His posturings, as Winter points out, are purely absurd, and an inflated ego shouldn't be equated with tragic pride or a noble character. Winter saw, besides, that Viola is as central to *Twelfth Night* as Malvolio. "Yet Malvolio is not the central image in the comedy, to the exclusion of Viola," he wrote. "If the humour crystallises around him, the tender loveliness, the poetic beauty, the ardent unselfish emotion, the exquisite glee and radiant grace crystallise around her. Viola is Shakespeare's ideal of the patient idolatry and devoted, silent self-sacrifice of perfect love."

This was an opinion held also by William Hazlitt, another romantic critic who commented, at about the time of Lamb that "The great and secret charm of *Twelfth Night* is the character of Viola. Much as we like catches and cakes and ale, there is something that we like better. We have a friendship for Sir Toby;

we patronize Sir Andrew; we have an understanding with the Clown, a sneaking kindness for Maria and her rogueries; we feel a regard for Malvolio, and sympathize with his gravity his smiles, his cross garters, his yellow stockings, and imprisonment in the stock. But there is something that excites in us a stronger feeling than all this-it is Viola's confession of her love."

MODERN CRITICS

Nearer our own day, critics like the Danish Georg Brandes, the British Sir Edmund Chambers and the American Mark Van Doren have had useful and perceptive ideas about the **theme**, structure, and unity of *Twelfth Night*. Both Brandes and Chambers, interestingly enough, compare it to *As You Like It*, its immediate comic predecessor. Writes Brandes: "*Twelfth Night* is perhaps the most graceful and harmonious comedy Shakespeare ever wrote. It is certainly that in which all the notes the poet strikes, the note of seriousness and of raillery, of passion, of tenderness, and of laughter, blend in the richest and fullest concord. It is like a symphony in which no strain can be dispensed with, or like a picture veiled in a golden haze, into which all the colors resolve themselves. The play does not overflow with wit and gaiety like its predecessor, *As You Like It*. We feel that Shakespeare's joy of life has culminated and is about to pass over into melancholy; but there is far more unity in it than in *As You Like It*, and it is a great deal more dramatic." And Sir Edmund Chambers notes that "the parallels between [the two plays] are easy to draw. The ordered gardens of the Boccaccio-like villa in Illyria and the pastoral glades of the forest of Arden serve equally well for images of that civilized and sheltered society wherein alone, according to Meredith, comedy obtains its real scope; and each lends an appropriate setting to those wilful departures from the way of right reason which it is the proper and special mission of comedy to correct . . . *As You Like It* is the comedy of the romantics, of the imagination which runs away with the facts of life and frames impossible ideals on the extravagant assumption that human nature in a forest is something wholly different from human nature in a court. *Twelfth Night* in its turn is the comedy of the sentimentalists, of the tendency of minds pent in the artificial atmosphere of cities to a spiritual self-deception, whereby they indulge in the expression of emotions not because they really have them, but because they have come to be regarded by themselves or others as modish or delightful emotions to have."

Mark Van Doren, perhaps most interestingly of all, has pointed out a parallel with *The Merchant of Venice*. "If so absorbing a masterpiece as *Twelfth Night*," he writes, "permits the reader to keep any other play in his mind while he reads, that play is *The Merchant of Venice*. Once again Shakespeare has built a world out of music and melancholy, and once again this world is threatened by an alien voice. The opposition of Malvolio to Orsino and his class parallels the opposition of Shylock to Antonio and his friends. The parallel is not precise, and the contrast is more subtly contrived; Shakespeare holds the balance in a more delicate hand, so that the ejection of Malvolio is perhaps less painful to our sense of justice than the punishments heaped upon Shylock until he is crushed under their weight. But the parallel exists, and nothing provides a nicer opportunity for studying the way in which Shakespeare, returning to a congenial **theme**, could ripen and enrich it." This comparison of Malvolio to Shylock (who was also often considered a "tragic" figure) reminds us again of Manningham's early emphasis on the steward, as well as-perhaps even more-of Lamb's insistence on Malvolio's basic nobility. In thus stressing the seriousness of that "mad" egotist, however, Van Doren seem to be taking quite a divergent route from most modern critics, who have more consistently pointed out the vanity, self-deception and absurdity of all the characters in *Twelfth Night*, including Malvolio.

Lately, too, there have been a number of scholarly studies of *Twelfth Night*, its sources and its audience, of which the foremost is probably Leslie Hotson's full-length *The First Night of Twelfth Night*. Hotson argues that *Twelfth Night* was first performed before Queen Elizabeth in January of 1600-1601, and that it therefore contains many personal and topical allusions. For instance, he claims that Malvolio was based in part on the character of Sir John Knollys, the Queen's Comptroller, and that Orsino, the Duke of Illyria, was based on a reference to a certain Italian Duke Orsino who was at that time visiting the English court. Whatever the truth of Hotson's theories, they make for fascinating reading, and every student of the play should become familiar with his book.

In general, then, though *Twelfth Night* doesn't lend itself to the kind of intensive analysis that most of Shakespeare's major tragedies have been subjected to, it has inspired a varied and fruitful body of criticism. Where earlier critics seemed to concentrate the most on the characters in the drama, especially Malvolio and Viola, modern thinkers have emphasized the **theme** and structure of the play, finding it, like Van Doren, predominantly "musical-melancholy" and, like Chambers and Brandes, built up out of an intricate series of relationships into a penetrating commentary on the paradoxes and pitfalls of self-love.

TWELFTH NIGHT

ESSAY QUESTIONS AND ANSWERS

Question: Discuss the **theme** of egotism, or "self-love" in *Twelfth Night*.

Answer: Some form of egotism-vanity, self-absorption, overweening ambition, etc. - is the basic fault of almost every character in *Twelfth Night*. Indeed, only Viola, along with such minor characters as Sebastian, Antonio, Fabian and perhaps Maria, seems to be entirely free of this quality. Malvolio, of course, is as we know "sick of self-love." His grotesque egotism leads him to believe that his ambition to become Olivia's husband is a reasonable one, and within the realm of possibility, when in fact it is absurd. Thus it is his self-love which is directly responsible for his downfall: his silly behavior with regard to Maria's letter and his subsequent "madness" and imprisonment. Orsino, too, though ostensibly a much nobler and more dignified personage than Malvolio, is in a sense "sick of self-love." His egotism leads him to believe that his shallow, pretentious "passion" for Olivia is a profound emotion, and that "there is no woman's sides/ Can bide the beating of so strong a passion/ As love doth give my heart . . ." Self-absorbed and drowned in melancholy, the Duke is merely in love with love, kept by his own egotism from experiencing the real thing until, from the example of Viola's selfless devotion, he learns what true love is.

Olivia - despite her wit, beauty and aristocratic bearing - is also driven by self-love. Her exaggerated grief for her brother, for one thing, seems to be based mainly on an egotistical desire for self-dramatization, especially when we compare it with Viola's typically unostentatious sorrow. Furthermore, her "pride," he unsympathetic coldness to Orsino, and her extravagant impulsiveness in the pursuit of "Cesario," are all unmistakable signs of egotism and vanity. Vanity, even more than self-absorption, is Sir Andrew Aguecheek's cardinal fault. It is his egotistical vanity which is piqued by Viola's success with Olivia, and it was certainly his ridiculous vanity which enabled him to think he ever had a chance with the lovely Countess in the first place. Even Sir Toby and Feste - though to a lesser degree than the others-suffer from egotism. What else, after all, is Toby's prankish desire to manipulate the lives of others through his tricks and jokes but a form of unbridled egotism? And surely his monstrous gluttony and endless imbibing are further signs of self-absorption. As for Feste, his furious reaction to Malvolio's insults can't be attributed to mere professional pride. It is egotism, and vanity, of a deeper and bitterer order that drives the jester on, even to the end of the play, to seek a petty revenge.

Question: Why can the predominating tone of *Twelfth Night*, especially the romantic plot, be called "musical-melancholy?"

Answer: For one thing, *Twelfth Night* is probably Shakespeare's most musical play. As G. B. Harrison has pointed out, "it not only begins with music, the whole play is an elaborate composition." Thus the scenes of merrymaking and the scenes of melancholy are carefully placed to balance and contrast with each other, just as the fast and slow movements of a symphony might be. Furthermore, the rich, eloquent language of the serious characters is consistently grave, melodious and lyrical-more so perhaps than in any other Shakespeare comedy but *The Tempest*. Finally, of course, as Harrison mentioned, the play is literally interwoven with real music, beginning and ending on a note of song-with a number of sad solos for Feste, and drinking songs for Toby and company in between.

Feste's sad solos-as well as the grave melody of much of the language-make the word "melancholy" also applicable to *Twelfth Night*. Orsino, Viola and Olivia are all consumed with melancholy-Orsino with the egotistical melancholy of his passion for Olivia; Olivia with the melodramatic melancholy of her grief for her brother and her love for "Cesario;" and Viola with the deeper, more sincere, "green and yellow melancholy" of her seemingly hopeless devotion to Orsino. And music feeds the melancholy of all three: Orsino consistently calls for it; Olivia, too, can undoubtedly be moved by it (though she doesn't make a point of it as Orsino does); and Viola, from the passionate depths of her "secret" heart, exclaims that Feste's song "gives a very echo to the seat where love is throned." Indeed, it is this universal melancholy of the serious characters which Fabian is parodying when he jokingly remarks "If I lose a scruple of this sport, let me be boiled to death with melancholy."

Question: In what ways are most of the comic characters **satires** on conventional Elizabethan personality types?

Answer: Though Orsino and Olivia-with their extravagant egotism and melancholy-may be said in some sense to be parodies of aristocrats, they aren't nearly such faithful social portraits as Malvolio, Toby, Andrew, Maria, Feste and Fabian are. Malvolio, of course, is at least in part a **satire** on the

Puritan, with his priggish, pompous, gloomily efficient manners and morals. More, he's a type of the self-made man, the rising middle-class tradesman or entrepreneur, with all his inevitable faults of ambition, hypocrisy, pride and humorlessness-as well as his virtues of logic, efficiency, honesty and punctuality. But if Malvolio represents the new social order, Sir Toby and the others are representatives of the old order, which is perhaps why they resent Olivia's steward so intensely. Toby, certainly, is a typical, fat, jolly, lazy, merrymaking English knight-just as Sir John Falstaff, in the *Henry IV* plays was. And like that other typical knight, Toby is hard-drinking, boisterous, brawling, always ready to pass the time with a prank or joke, and almost always a little unscrupulous, especially in his treatment of Sir Andrew.

But if Toby is the typical jolly knight, Andrew is the typical "weakminded" hanger-on, a caricature of the cowardly fool or "knave" who was so much despised by the Elizabethans. Neither his wealth, nor his willingness to go along with any gag, redeem him. In the end, he's no more than a "knave, a gull." Maria, of course, is the standard shrewd servingwoman, a type as common in romantic comedies like *Twelfth Night* as in real life. Fond of fun and with sly private designs of her own (in this case on Sir Toby) she could be encountered in any Elizabethan tavern (cf. Mistress Quickly in the *Henry IV* plays) or even, as here, in any great household. As for Feste and Fabian - the first is a typical jester, with a ready professional pride and frank, wittily put opinions of everyone around him, while the second is a typical upper-level servant, not so self-important as Malvolio but just genial and congenial enough to be always in the good graces of his masters. Indeed, he stands in relation to the old, inefficient merrymaking servant class, much as Sir Toby does to the declining class of carousing aristocrats.

Question: How does the device of mistaken identity trigger the whole plot of *Twelfth Night*?

Answer: Mistaken identity, frequently based on the confusion of twins of different sexes, has been a favorite device of comic dramatists from the time of the Roman playwright Plautus. In the Renaissance the device became especially popular - and Shakespeare used it often, in the *Comedy of Errors* and *Two Gentlemen of Verona* as well as *Twelfth Night*. In *Twelfth Night*, of course, the whole play is based on Viola's being disguised as "Cesario." This enables Olivia to fall, apparently hopelessly, in love with her - and it enables her to fall hopelessly in love with Orsino. No one can respond to anyone else's passion in this mixed-up triangle because Viola's true sex isn't known. Later, when Sebastian appears on the scene, mistaken identity again becomes of paramount importance-in this case, in resolving the plot complications it caused in the first place. At last Olivia can get married to the "man" she loves - "Cesario," now, of course, really Sebastian and therefore able to return her feelings. And at last Viola can reveal her true identity, and in her "woman's weeds" win the heart of Orsino.

But besides triggering the romantic plot, mistaken identity motivates a good part of the comic plot-particularly that section concerned with the duel between Andrew and Viola. If Viola hadn't, to begin with, been mistaken for a boy by Olivia, then Andrew's jealousy would never have been aroused; and if Andrew himself didn't also imagine her a boy, he'd never have challenged her to a duel. Furthermore, if Andrew hadn't challenged her to a duel, Antonio might never have intervened, thinking she was Sebastian. Again, in the end, Sebastian's presence resolves the whole affair. When Toby and Andrew mistake him for Viola, they're soundly beaten, as they deserve to be, and this episode too comes to a happy conclusion.

Finally, one might even claim that mistaken identity plays a part in the important Malvolio sub-plot, since the unfortunate steward is led by Maria to mistake her identity (her words and handwriting in the "anonymous" love-letter) for Olivia's. Later, too, when he's been imprisoned as a lunatic, the unhappy man mistakes Feste for "Sir Topas," the priest. Indeed, such misrule - the misrule of the *Twelfth Night* festivities - as evidenced in a wealth of mistaken identities-is practically universal in this play!

Question: What part does "madness" play in this work?

Answer: Madness seems to be the chief quality of Shakespeare's Illyria, where *Twelfth Night* "misrule" is the order of the day, mistaken identity is common, and everything is topsy-turvy. "Are all the people mad?" asks the eminently sane Sebastian, when he's been mistaken by a third character for "Cesario." And later, after Olivia has made her first romantic advances to him, he wonders if he's mad or dreaming, conjecturing that "I am mad or else the lady's mad." Antonio, too, is accused of madness: when Viola denies knowing him after he's asked her for his purse, and he complains of her ingratitude, thinking she's Sebastian, the officers impatiently exclaim "The man grows mad." Of course, the chief case of madness in the play is Malvolio-whose madness consists not only of the lunatic frenzy into which Maria's letter throws him, but also of his overweening egotism and ambition. But even Olivia, for all her dignity and importance, behaves in *Twelfth Night* with a kind of madness. As she herself points out, discussing Malvolio, "I am as mad as he/ If sad and merry madness equal be." Olivia's melancholy, like Orsino's, is extravagant and melodramatic, because unrelated to reality - and hence mad. In this sense Sir Andrew's deluded vanity and Toby's drunken revelry are also signs of madness. Indeed, perhaps the only major characters who aren't mad are

Viola-whose melancholy has a real cause and is therefore sane - and Feste, beneath whose "foolery' and madcap wit there's such a core of sense and sanity that the equally rational Viola can remark "This fellow is wise enough to play the fool" - recognizing a wisdom which most of the other characters, being naturally fools and madmen, lack.

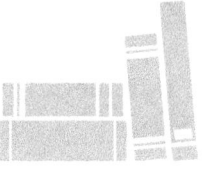

BIBLIOGRAPHY

A good research paper on *Twelfth Night* should be based on an accurate text of the play with thorough notes. Probably the best and most useful modern text is the hardcover New Arden Edition, edited by J. B. Leishman and published by the Harvard University Press. There are also a number of good paperback editions; one of the finest is certainly the Bantam Shakespeare Commemoration Edition, edited by Oscar James Campbell, Alfred Rothschild and Stuart Vaughan. In addition to a reliable text of the play, with a helpful marginal gloss, it contains much useful background material, including comments by the editors on Shakespeare's life and times and Shakespeare's theatre as well as (most welcome of all) a historical sampling of critical opinion about *Twelfth Night*.

Though countless books have been written about Shakespeare's life and works, not too much has been produced specifically about *Twelfth Night*. Much of what there is, however, is interesting and illuminating. Very often, furthermore, general works on Shakespeare-his theater, his life, his comedies-will yield ideas for papers that deal solely with *Twelfth Night*. Following is a selected list of valuable criticism, arranged alphabetically by author within some key research topics.

TWELFTH NIGHT

Questions to consider: How is the plot of *Twelfth Night* organized? Is it unified or not? What balancing elements does the playwright supply? What is the work's **theme**? What were some of Shakespeare's main sources for his plot.

Archer, William. "The Two Twelfth Nights." *Fortnightly Review*, CX (1918).

Bullough, Geoffrey, ed. *Narrative and Dramatic Sources of Shakespeare.* Vol. II. London and New York, 1958. Contains the chief sources of *Twelfth Night*, and an excellent introduction on the dating of the play, as well as on Shakespeare's use of his sources.

Draper, John W. *The Twelfth Night of Shakespeare's Audience.* London; Oxford University Press, 1950. A thorough-going discussion of the characters and situations in relation to their Elizabethan originals.

Hotson, Leslie. *The First Night of Twelfth Night.* London: Rupert Hart-Davis, 1954. A scholarly theory about the first performance of the play, and how its audience affected its writing.

Musechke, P. and Fleisher, J. "Jonsonian Elements in the Comic Underplot of *Twelfth Night.*" *PMLA*, XLVIII (1933).

Priestley, J. B. "The Illyrians." *The English Comic Characters*. London, 1925.

Symons, Arthur. "*Twelfth Night.*" *Studies in the Elizabethan Drama.* London, 1920. Commentary by a distinguished early modern critic.

Tilley, M. P. "The Organic Unity of *Twelfth Night.*" *PMLA*, XXIX (1914), 550-556.

Williams, Porter, Jr. "Mistakes in *Twelfth Night* and their Resolution: A Study of Some Relationships of Plot and Theme." *PMLA*, LXXVL (1962), 193-199. A brief, useful, contemporary analysis of the structure of the play.

THE CHARACTER OF MALVOLIO

Questions to consider: How important a role does Malvolio play in *Twelfth Night*? Is he chiefly a serious or a comic character? What is his major flaw? What Elizabethan type or types did Shakespeare satirize in him? Was he modeled on any specific person of the day, and if so, on whom?

Archer, William. "*Twelfth Night* at the Lyceum." *Macmillan's Magazine* (August, 1884). (Reprinted in the Bantam edition of *Twelfth Night.*) Includes an interesting study of Malvolio as a character.

Gollancz, Sir Israel. "Malvolio." *A Book of Homage to Shakespeare.* London, 1916.

Hotson, Leslie. *The First Night of Twelfth Night.* London, Rupert, Hart-Davis, 1954. Contains a chapter conjecturing that Malvolio's character was based on that of Sir John Knollys, the Queen's Comptroller.

Lamb, Charles. "On Some of the Old Actors." *The Essays of Elia.* London, 1811. (Reprinted in the Bantam edition of *Twelfth Night.*) Includes a famous discussion of Malvolio's essential seriousness and "austerity."

Seiden, Melvin. "Malvolio Reconsidered." *University of Kansas City Review*, XXVIII (1960), 105-114.

Thaler, A. "The Original Malvolio?" *Shakespeare Assoc. Bulletin*, VII (1932).

Van Doren, Mark. "*Twelfth Night.*" Shakespeare. New York, 1953. (reprinted in Bantam *Twelfth Night.*) Contains an interesting comparison of Malvolio to Shylock.

Winter, William. "The Characters of *Twelfth Night* on the stage." Shadows of the Stage, 3rd series. 1895. (reprinted in the Bantam edition of *Twelfth Night.*)

Wright, L. B. "A Conduct Book for Malvolio." *Studies in Philology*, XXXI (1934), 115-132.

THE ROLE OF FESTE

Questions to consider: What was the role of the fool in Shakespeare's plays? Who was the original of Feste? What is the function of Feste in *Twelfth Night*?

Bradley, A. C. "Feste the Jester." *A Miscellany.* New York, 1929.

Downer, Alan S. "Feste's Night." *College English*, XIII (1952), 258-265.

Goldsmith, Robert H. *Wise Fools in Shakespeare.* East Lansing: Michigan State University Press, 1955

Hotson, Leslie. *Shakespeare's Motley.* London, 1952. A study of Elizabethan jesters which illuminates the character of Feste. Includes a description of Robert Armin, for whom the part was originally written.

Welsford, Enid, *The Fool.* New York: Doubleday Anchor, 1961. Paperback. The definitive work on the subject.

THE PLACE OF MUSIC

Questions to consider: How did Shakespeare use music in *Twelfth Night?* Why is it often considered his "most musical work?" To what extent were his songs based on popular songs of the day?

Auden, W. H. Greenberg, Noah & Kallman, Chester, ed. *An Elizlbethan Song Book.* New York: Doubleday Anchor, 1955. Paperback. Contains words and music of many Elizabethan popular songs.

Bridge, Frederick. "O Mistress Mine": *Shakespearean Music in the Plays and Early Operas.* London, 1923.

Noble, Richmond, *Shakespeare's Use of Song*, with the text of the principal songs. Oxford: Oxford University Press, 1923.

Sternfield, F. W. "Shakespeare's Use of Popular Song," Elizabethan and Jacobean Studies in *Shakespeare's Songs, **Sonnets** and Poems." Shakespeare Survey*, XV (1962), 1-10.

www.ingramcontent.com/pod-product-compliance
Lightning Source LLC
LaVergne TN
LVHW011709060526
838200LV00051B/2830